The Remodeler's Guide to
MAKING & MANAGING MONEY

A common sense approach to
optimizing compensation & profit

Linda W. Case

Remodelers
ADVANTAGE
Proven Business Solutions

Remodelers Advantage, Inc. • Silver Spring, Maryland

The Remodeler's Guide to
MAKING & MANAGING MONEY

A common sense approach to optimizing compensation & profit

Remodelers
ADVANTAGE
Proven Business Solutions

Also by Linda Case:

Marketing for Remodelers:
Leads for Building Business

Remodelers Business Basics

Design Build for Remodelers,
Custom Builders and Architects

Remodeling Production
with Walter Stoeppelwerth

The Remodeler's Marketing PowerPak
with Victoria L. Downing

The Remodeler's Guide to

MAKING & MANAGING MONEY

By Linda W. Case

Published by:

Remodelers
ADVANTAGE
Proven Business Solutions

Remodelers Advantage, Inc.
9834 Capitol View Avenue
Silver Spring, MD 20910 U.S.A.

Copyright © 1996 by Linda W. Case
First Printing 1996

Printed in the United States of America.
Library of Congress Catalog Card Number 95-92481
ISBN: 0-9648587-4-6

Cover & book design by Cristina Diez de Medina, A Scribbler's Press

Thank you!

The manuscript for this book was reviewed by a dozen experts from remodeling businesses of all sizes and the financial world. Their comments saved me from many pitfalls and errors. Certainly, their input and changes have saved you from boredom.

Many thanks to my associate, Victoria Downing, whose quick pencil refines and edits with expertise. Also to my son, Charles Case, who made many important changes, and to the following generous people:

Elizabeth Brady, *Anthony Wilder Design Build,* Bethesda, MD

David Brennan, *Summit Construction Services,* Southington, CT

Ed Castle, *E. M. Castle Construction,* Silver Spring, MD

Hobie Iselin, *Construct Associates,* Northampton, MA

Harvey Levin, *Dial One Wathen Construction,*
Indianapolis, IN

Kevin Kalman, *Kalman Construction Corp.,*
Nantucket, MA

Steve Maltzman, CPA, *Construction Accounting Service,* Colton, CA

Gail Pasternak, CPA, *C.W. Amos, Certified Public Accountants and Business Consultants,* Bethesda, MD

Brian Reid, *Reid's Remodeling,*
Jamestown, RI

All the examples in this book are real —
adapted from six generous remodelers
across the country. Here's a big thank you
from all of us to:

Matt Davitt, *Davitt Woodworks, Inc.,*
North Kingstown, RI

David DiGiorgi, *DiGiorgi Roofing & Siding,*
Seymour, CT

Jim Kuhn, *Consolidated Construction Group,*
St. Louis, MO

Jerry Roth, *G. M. Roth Design Remodeling,*
Nashua, NH

Jake Schloegel, *Schloegel Contracting Co. Inc.,*
Kansas City, MO

Jim Strite, *Strite Remodeling,*
Boise, ID

Index

Introduction

If I had a penny for every remodeler who felt just a little guilty at the prospect of pricing jobs at the level needed to produce a good owner's salary plus profit for the company, my prosperous retirement would be assured.

If I had a nickel for every remodeler who, when asked how good a financial manager they were, said "I just leave that to the bookkeeper," I'd be very wealthy.

If you added a dime for every company I met that makes do with ill-prepared bookkeepers and inexperienced and uninterested accountants, I'd own an island in some sunny climate.

Why is there a mystique—an anxiety—about making and managing money among remodelers? A New England remodeler who struggles with his ability to understand financial reports explains "fear of the unknown—no matter how irrational—is a real block in its ability to paralyze your action."

As a remodeler, you work with numbers every day. Don't be afraid of numbers. Anyone who can do extensive and exhaustive estimates for jobs like you do, has all the ability needed to understand—and manage—straightforward financial reports. If financial reports make you nervous, this is the book for you. Our goal is to make those numbers and those financial reports as friendly and helpful as Smokey the Bear!

Why Bother?

Why bother with the information in this book? In a word you bother because of money. You want money for yourself and you want money for your company.

Edward Welles writes in the September, 1995, INC. magazine "...it's well documented that the time-tested way to lasting wealth in America is to start your own company. Do it right and you get the lion's share of what your company earns. Do it really right and you build up some impressive equity that could one day turn into a goodly chunk of cash."

Maybe you feel guilty thinking about how much money your business can provide for you. It's up to you what you do with that money. You can give it to your favorite charity as actor Paul Newman does with the proceeds of his various food products. You can start a college fund for your three kids. You can tithe to your church. There is no doubt that the company that makes money consistently, creates long lasting jobs for its employees and creates the equity that allows it to deliver superb service to its clients.

Money is Made by Deliberate Action

Making money rarely happens by luck in a business. As Martin King writes in *Managing the Small Construction Business*, "We produce profits consciously, by taking specific actions. The production of profit requires experience, foresight, and planning—things that minimize uncertainty and risk." You plan for profit by budgeting and estimating and you monitor profit with regular financial reports.

No matter how exact your monthly financial reports, you can't make profit happen if you have not been able to sell the job at the proper price. However, if you planned well, if you've made a clear roadmap to profit (budget) for yourself, you can then turn your attention to bringing in your volume, your job costs and overhead on target. If you see they are off your projected numbers, you can take quick action to avert disaster. Profit results from good planning plus good managing.

Financial Terms

Like all fields, finance has special terms and language meant to be understood by those insiders who work in that field. But then remodeling has its own special terms—muntins, soffits, returns, bridging—that are just as logical once you understand what they mean! So let's dig in and clear away any fog you might have.

Chapter 1

Owner/Investor Compensation

"Every morning, I get up and look through the Forbes (magazine) list of the richest people in America. If I'm not there, I go to work."

Humorist Robert Orben

 **It** is a rare remodeler who goes into this business because they are seeking riches. Far more common is the search for fulfillment and for serving others while being allowed to pursue their craft.

You may have started with a very humble goal. You were tired of working for others and "dancing to their tune." You wanted to work for yourself, do the job the way you thought it should be done. Your goal was to make as much money working for yourself as you were being paid at your last job. Your main benefits would be being your own boss, managing your own time and leaving the job looking the way you thought it should look. Truth was, many of you weren't really starting a business, you were creating a job for yourself.

But soon that job evolved into a business with employees, equipment, vehicles, insurance and many other responsibilities. Maybe it's time to reevaluate your income. After all, now you are both an employee of the company and an investor in the company. You want to look at yourself as playing both roles, no matter what the legal form of your company happens to be.

If your company is a sole proprietorship, all income left over after expenses is considered your income by the government. Is it enough income for the roles you perform in the company? As an employee you perform specific day-to-day work and as the investor you take the risk of losing any money that is invested in the company as well as the risk of a catastrophe tapping your personal funds. Let's evaluate what you should earn at a minimum in your company.

Your Salary

In 1994, I took one long continuous survey of what remodelers pay themselves. Thousands of remodelers who took my seminars, anonymously filled out simple survey forms. The results were depressing. When I reviewed the range of pay for three volume levels (small companies to $250,000, medium companies to $750,000 and large companies above $750,000), the vast majority of remodelers were woefully underpaid.

But the top end of the income range at each volume level was quite well paid. So while the bad news is that most remodelers pay themselves too little, the good news is that we know that you can be well paid working for your own company at every volume level.

Figuring Minimum Pay

So we won't talk about what "most remodelers" pay themselves because that will be a bad example and depress us. Here's how I recommend you figure out your minimum pay. First, answer these two questions:

1. Ten percent of my total company volume annually is

   $_____.

2. A top lead carpenter in my area makes

   $_____ annually. Add $5000 to this

   amount = $_____.

Then, use the result of either 1 or 2—whichever is higher —as a base for your salary.

Case Study A California remodeler has an annual volume of $350,000 and pays his/her top lead carpenter $25 an hour. When we apply the 10% of volume rule, the remodeler would be paid $35,000. However, the $25 an hour carpenter receives $50,000 a year in pay (to get annual pay from hourly, multiply by 2000 hours). When we add $5000 to that, the remodeler should pay himself/herself $55,000 minimum. By using the second rule, we see that the pay is $20,000 more than by the first rule.

These are minimums. You are encouraged to pay yourself more. However, if you pay yourself less, you are only playing at business. You do not have a real business that supports you. You would be able to walk into another firm, work 45-50 hours a week and get more pay with fewer headaches. If you underpay yourself, you'll get discouraged, work harder and longer and burn out. And then you'll go work for another remodeler.

Partners' Salaries

It is more difficult to recommend salaries for two or three partners. The best procedure is to follow the rules above for setting a salary for the first partner and then add market rate salaries for the other partner or partners. That becomes a pot of money to split between the partners. In other words if the California remodeler in the example above had a partner who worked on the job as lead carpenter, you could combine the $55,000 for the first partner with the $50,000 the lead carpenter partner would make at market rate, and each would receive $52,500 as a salary.

$$\frac{\$55,000 + \$50,000}{2} = \frac{\$105,000}{2} = \$52,500$$

However, sometimes the roles of partners are of very unequal worth in the marketplace. As a company grows, the market rate salaries for the salesperson's job, the production manager's job, and the carpenter's job become much more unequal. In this case, some partnerships continue to keep the salaries equal and some do not. Also, partners may want or need to work a significantly different number of hours and you may want to take that into account as you set salaries.

Outside Input

INC. magazine studied company owner salaries for those on their prestigious INC. 500 list of fastest growing private companies over the previous five years. They found a huge divergence in owner compensation.

■ Fifty percent of the company owners consulted no one in setting their compensation—they just set it.

▦ Those who did consult others read published surveys, talked with accountants, boards, trade associations, spouses, compensation experts or lawyers.

▦ Eighty percent surveyed company needs when setting their salary and thirty-nine percent felt their pay was below market rate.

▦ Thirty-seven percent felt their compensation was about right.

▦ Sixty-six percent of those owners surveyed noted that a bonus was part of their pay and for a third of the owners, bonus comprised at least twenty-five percent of their pay.

COMPENSATION SINS

In INC.'s report on their owner compensation study (September, 1995, issue), they listed five cardinal sins of CEO compensation—four of which are pertinent here:

1. Cheating yourself (and your family) with too little pay when your company is young. As John Greene, president of Custom Transportation Service in Braintree, MA, notes "If you treat yourself as an employee, and pay yourself properly from the get-go, you can't go wrong."

2. Gouging the company by paying yourself too much.

3. Basing your income on bad numbers that make you feel your company is fatter than it is.

4. Getting bogged down with too many benefits for yourself and your employees. These fixed expenses are not easy to take away if your company takes a dive.

Your Benefits

Stephen Covey, the business guru and author of *The Seven Habits of Highly Effective People*, would call you a "goose." And Covey would not be insulting you. In his book he retells Aesop's fable of the impoverished farmer who has a pet goose. One day the farmer discovers a golden egg in the nest. Day after day the goose lays these precious golden eggs. The farmer soon becomes greedy and impatient. He decides to kill the goose so that he can get all the eggs at once. But when he cuts open his former pet, he finds no eggs at all. Because of his action, he has no goose and no more golden eggs. He soon falls back into poverty.

You are the goose that lays the golden eggs for your business. If you were to sicken and die, your business would likely sicken and die. Therefore, your business must treat you kindly, feed you well, keep you happy — if you are to continue to produce. If the business runs you into the ground with overwork and poor care, you will no longer have the talent, creativity and leadership that makes you that golden egg producer. So we better take good care of you by giving you not only a good salary but also good benefits.

TYPICAL BENEFITS. Remodelers usually give themselves family health insurance, a vehicle, possibly disability insurance, life insurance and a retirement program.

VACATION. You should receive (and use) an absolute minimum of two weeks yearly. A number of remodelers take up to six weeks a year. For the small company owner, it takes considerable preparation to be able to go away on two one-week vacations. Warn all homeowners whose jobs span your vacation time that you'll be gone. If you have personnel, this is a chance to get them ready to take some responsibility. Remodeler after remodeler has told me, "my employees did so much better than I expected!" The world will not break down because you are on vacation. However, you will break down if you don't take vacations.

HOURS. Keep your hours to an average of 50-55. If you are consistently working more than this, you are headed for burnout. Remodelers who sell may have to move their selling into the daylight hours. Let others pick up materials—but only when they can't be ordered ahead. You may have to outsource design and other tasks. If you are determined to do it, you can—just like thousands of other remodelers have reduced their hours.

There's a second powerful benefit to reducing your hours. Studies show that workers are most creative when they are not at their job. Many businesspeople do their best problem solving in the shower, while boating or fishing, or when they exercise. We also know that you're more likely to create a happy balance between your personal life and business life when you work reasonable hours. Hopefully, you'll use your time off to exercise, read and enjoy family activities. You'll keep your body and soul in good shape.

Role in Company

There is an important benefit that only you can give yourself—being sure that you spend at least 50% of your working time doing what you really like to do. (Every job has many tasks, surrounding the enjoyed roles, that just have to be done. For instance, estimating may be work you dislike while you enjoy selling. Or managing personnel may bore you while you enjoy doing carpentry work.) But sometimes, as your company grows, you find that you have taken on roles that give you little pleasure.

What do you like to do best—design, sell, manage production, administrate, or work on the job? When I ask remodelers this question, they know right away. Unfortunately, as a company grows, the owner may be pulled away into spending all her time doing other tasks. Let's be sure you spend at least 50 percent of your time in the role you like. That will keep you much happier at work.

The Ethics of Those "Hidden" Benefits

It's rare to listen to a tape or read a book about owner pay and benefits without hearing a laughing reference to "hidden" benefits to the remodeler. These often involve remodeling your home, or hardware goodies for your personal use that are hidden in your job costs and charged to the company, getting a sub to repair the second floor bathroom and invoicing the repair to the Gelman job.

Consider what your policy is on these backdoor benefits. What are your personal beliefs and ethics? How do your business practices fit with your personal beliefs? I once heard a company owner explain how she made a decision when tempted to cut a corner. She said "I just apply the *New York Times* rule. I picture what I'm thinking about doing as a headline in the *New York Times*. Most of the time, my proposed action just doesn't pass this test."

There's another issue to think about. It's the "what message does this send to my employees and my subs?" rule. What is the meaning of honesty in your company? Each of us would define honesty slightly differently when we got to the what-ifs. Is it okay to take a pen from work and keep it at home? Is it okay to take a screwdriver? How about an expensive power tool? Wherever you draw the line, I believe you must—for your own protection—send a message of scrupulous honesty to your personnel.

There is still a third issue to "hidden" benefits. How accurate will your financial reports be if you play these games? Today, as I write this, I received a call from a western remodeler who asked for input on his profit and loss statement. He agreed to fax it to me but warned "It doesn't show the true volume because I do some of my jobs for cash...and the costs are inflated because of some personal items I've bought on the company tab." It would be very difficult to help him.

Your Investor/Risk-taker Return

Up to now we've been talking about the pay and benefits you deserve as the most important worker in your company. Now let's focus on the return you should get as an investor and risk taker in your company. Perhaps you've left $25,000 in as retained earnings to run the company, or you invested $10,000 to get the company started. You should be earning a return on that money. After all, if you had invested that money elsewhere, it would be earning additional money for you—probably with a lot less risk.

"If a company...is profitable but earns a lower return than a U.S. Treasury bond, why should money be invested in such a business, an inherently risky decision, when more could be made in the risk-free bond?" asks Robert Finney, *Every Manager's Guide to Business Finance*.

In an upcoming chapter on Balance Sheets, there is a Return on Equity ratio that will help you calculate your return as an investor. Few remodelers get wealthy from their remodeling businesses. Some get wealthy by investing the money generated by remodeling in land, buildings, other businesses. Take your return out of the company and consider building some diversification by investing it elsewhere.

Don't settle for only a "job" in your company. Work to achieve a net profit of 10% of your gross sales which will be your "return." This is over-and-above your salary. All companies are in business to produce this return for their investors, who are risking their money every day. Your company should do the same.

You Pay Yourself

We've been reviewing logical compensation and benefits. No one else will earn the money to pay for them—you must. If, for a second, you feel guilt at earning a good return, take a lesson from the legendary New York Yankee, Babe Ruth. During the Depression, Ruth was asked to take a pay cut but he held out for his $80,000 salary. One club official protested, "But that's more money than Hoover got for being president last year."

"I know," said Babe Ruth, "but I had a better year."

You have to make those "better years" happen so you can share in the prosperity. That's what this book is all about.

CHAPTER ONE CHECK-UP

1. According to this chapter, what minimum salary would a Midwest remodeler with $500,000 in volume and a carpenter earning $14 an hour, pay himself?

2. Company owners should be paid both as employees of the company and as investor/risktakers.

   ☐ True   ☐ False

3. The values and ethics you believe in personally don't necessarily fit into business decisions.

   ☐ True   ☐ False

4. While large volume remodelers can take a vacation, it's really not possible for small volume remodelers to go away for more than a day or two.

   ☐ True   ☐ False

5. A 50-55 hour week seems to help prevent burnout in remodelers.

   ☐ True   ☐ False

6. Your business should produce a 10% net profit over-and-above your salary.

   ☐ True   ☐ False

CHECK YOUR ANSWERS ON THE NEXT PAGE → → →

ANSWERS

1. $50,000 or 10% of his volume.

2. True. Company owners should be paid both as employees of the company and as investor/risktakers.

3. False. It's best to keep your business ethics consistent with your personal ethics.

4. False. All remodelers can go on vacation if it's important to them.

5. True. While many remodelers work up to 100 hours a week, keeping to a 50-55 hour week is possible and helps prevent burnout.

6. True. Your business should produce enough money to pay you well and produce a 10% net profit.

Chapter 2

Getting the Right Information

"People who run companies know there are really only two critical factors in business. One is to make money and the other is to generate cash. As long as you do those two things, your company is going to be OK, even if you make mistakes along the way."

Jack Stack, <u>The Great Game of Business</u>

If you have flown recently, you probably looked into the cockpit as you entered the airplane. Isn't the amount of instrumentation overwhelming? Why are all those dials and readouts there? After all, why couldn't the pilot make do with just one light that flashes if the plane is in trouble? They could, but as we'll see below, they wouldn't have the right information about the right areas of operation at the right time.

Remodelers are using this "flashing red light" system when they try to manage their companies with their checkbook as their only tool. They have one flashing red light (an empty bank account) that says "feed me!" But why does the checkbook need money? Is it because volume is too low, markup is too little, job costs are too high, overhead is uncontrolled.....?

When the bank account is empty, there's no time to diagnose. Instead you rush to find money to deposit. Wherever the money comes from—and it may even be the downpayment from the next job—you relax once you can cover your outstanding checks. This can become a "permanently painful way of doing business" as one remodeler warns. You have removed the warning symptom temporarily. Yet you have taken no action to diagnose and treat the underlying illness. Your business is just as sick as it was before—perhaps even sicker.

Using Information Preventatively

The pilot has all those dials because he/she needs fast, targeted information. That information will be used preventively to diagnose oncoming problems and solve them before they become life threatening. If a catastrophe happens anyway, those instruments will provide information that diagnoses where the problem is, out of hundreds or thousands of potential causes, so that the pilot can take quick, precise action against the true cause.

Your financial reports are your company's instrumentation:

- They provide critical information on what is happening.
- They help you control the operation of your company.
- They allow you to take preventative action when a negative trend is developing.
- They quickly pinpoint trouble spots in case of serious difficulty so that you can take fast, targeted action.

INFORMATION: The types of financial reports we will review have been developed over many years and contain critical information in a universally agreed upon format. Who is this information for? It is for you. While the IRS will certainly want this information about your business, that is the secondary (although certainly necessary) reason it is collected.

CONTROL: Budgets, profit and loss statements, balance sheets, job costs are developed to help you manage your company. Budgets set goals. Profit and loss reports check how you are doing against those goals. Job estimates set goals while job costs report back your score—how you are doing against those goals. All help you to track when corrective action needs to be taken.

In addition the company has certain assets—cash, equipment, property, vehicles—and it's important that you know that those assets are being well used and safeguarded. Financial reports are the guides by which you monitor their condition.

PREVENTATIVE ACTION: By setting goals that will lead to profit, you create a tool to help you see when the company results have deviated from the roadmap you have created. By getting monthly reports, you are able to take early action to change a trend. For instance, you might see that job costs have gone up 5% over the last few months. You can then take action to turn this negative trend around and watch month by month, job cost by job cost, to be sure you have returned these costs to their projected level. Or your problem might be too little volume. You can scale back what you spend in overhead to fit your new volume or you can create an action plan for increasing volume quickly.

QUICK DIAGNOSIS OF TROUBLE SPOTS: One large job, one lost sale can dramatically affect company performance. If you are operating without much cushion, your financial reports will tell you what is happening and where the trouble is, so that you can mobilize everyone in the company to improve the problem area. You are able to diagnose quickly and accurately because of your reports.

Let's see what information you need and when you need it.

> *"Prevention is the best cure for financial problems. Setting up information flow so that problems are spotted early on is common sense."*
>
> David Bangs, <u>Financial Troubleshooting</u>

Questions and Answers

You have some very simple questions about money in your business. You want answers to questions like:

- Is my company making money? If so, how much? Could I make more?
- Are my finances getting better or worse?
- Will I have enough cash over the next month to handle payroll and my bills?
- Am I getting a good return on the money I've invested in my company?
- How are my job costs running compared to my estimates?
- Are my estimates accurate?

These are simple questions. But they are very important questions for staying alive and well in this challenging business. Wouldn't you think getting the answers would be just as simple? To the contrary, getting the answers to those questions can take reams of paper and many hours of data gathering each month.

So if you've been thinking that financial reports are for the birds (or the IRS, or your bank), you've been wrong. The main reason your company should generate financial reports is for you—the owner/investor, and for you—the manager. Let's review the five reports that will answer those "simple" questions you have. Every remodeling company owner must have—and be able to analyze—these reports to survive and thrive:

WHAT YOU NEED	WHEN YOU NEED IT
1. Profit and Loss Statement	monthly
2. Balance Sheet	monthly
3. Job Costs	at least monthly or timely at the end of each job
4. Cash Flow Projection	weekly
5. Company Budget	annually, realigned quarterly

Maybe you've been surviving without these reports. Maybe you've even been making money without these reports. Then you're like the pilot who flies without instrumentation but "hasn't crashed yet." What would you advise that pilot to do? I suspect you'd advise the pilot to get state-of-the-art instrumentation to assure his/her continuing safety. It's too late after the crash. That's why you've purchased this book and are reading it. You want state-of-the-art information to avoid a business crash.

Robert Finney in *Every Manager's Guide to Business Finance*, points out that "People begin their business careers primarily dealing with things. As they become managers, they begin to deal more with people than things. But, as they get promoted, they find their primary concern becomes money—how it is raised, invested, spent, tracked, controlled, and measured."

The next chapters will focus on each of the financial reports in greater depth. For now, let's check our knowledge on this chapter with a quiz.

NUMBER | DATE | DESCRIPTION OF TRANSACTION | PAYMENT/DEBIT | ✓ FEE | DEPOSIT/CREDIT | BALANCE

CHAPTER TWO CHECK-UP

1. Your financial reports are developed primarily for government reporting.

☐ True   ☐ False

2. List three of the five financial reports you need to run a company successfully:

a. _____

b. _____

c. _____

3. List two financial reports you should receive monthly:

a. _____

b. _____

4. Which financial document attempts to influence the future and is prepared annually but checked monthly or quarterly?

a. _____

5. Which financial report do you need to review weekly?

a. _____

CHECK YOUR ANSWERS ON THE NEXT PAGE → → →

Answers

1. False. Your financial reports are developed first and foremost to help you manage your company and only secondarily to provide information to the government.

2. The five financial reports you need to run a company success-fully are your profit and loss statement, your balance sheet, your job costs, your cash flow projection and your budget.

3. The two financial reports you should receive monthly are your profit and loss statement and your balance sheet.

4. Your budget attempts to influence the future and is prepared annually and checked monthly or quarterly.

5. You need to review your cash flow projection report each week.

Chapter 3

Your Profit & Loss Report

"Loss is to the business world what 'who forgot to fill the pool with water' is to the world of high diving."

Anonymous

he Profit & Loss Report (P & L) is also called the Income Statement or the Operating Statement. It shows what income was received or earned vs. what expenses or costs were incurred by the company for a given period. This report is the key to understanding your current operations.

The P & L gives you the financial score for the month and should be eagerly anticipated by all. First and foremost, the P & L shows how much net profit ("the bottom line") the company has earned—in other words, what is left from the income after the job cost and overhead money is spent.

Many remodelers think that this bottom line is all a Profit & Loss statement is good for. They glance hesitantly at the net profit line, grimace if it's in parentheses (because that means a loss) and smile if the amount is positive. However, even though their P & L may show a net profit bottom line, they complain that they can never actually find the money it says they should have!

What Your P & L Tells You

Your P & L is indeed an important scorecard but its most important function is to increase your control of your company by giving you the critical information that you need to run your company. It is a statement of your profitability and how the major areas of income and expense are working to deliver profit.

In your monthly Profit and Loss report you'll find the amount of the income that went to pay job costs and the amount that went to pay overhead. Hopefully, everyone in your company who is involved with sales or production wants to know how the job costs are coming in. Those responsible for overhead want to make sure that this area is on track and not consuming too much of the income. **The P & L is your starting point to diagnosing and changing any area that is holding your company back from its maximum performance.**

THE PROFIT & LOSS STATEMENT SIMPLY PUT...

Income – Job Costs = Gross Profit

Gross Profit – Overhead = Net Profit

THE P & L WITH A LITTLE MORE DETAIL

Your Profit and Loss Report tells a story — the story of your business over a period of time. Here's an example:

Craftsman Remodelers specializes in repairs. Over the past three months, they've been paid $24,300 by their customers to do a large number of repairs. To do those repairs it took $8495 in payroll costs, $4900 in materials and $2400 in electrical, plumbing, hvac and tile subcontractor costs.

Even after Craftsman has paid all of the above costs, they have to pay $6305 in overhead costs for the three months. If anything is left, it is profit. The owner is paid in job costs.

THE P & L REPORT:	3 Months
Income	$24,300
Job Costs	
Labor	8,495
Material	4,900
Subs	2,400
Gross Profit	$ 8,505
Overhead	6,305
Net Profit	2,200

A REAL PROFIT & LOSS STATEMENT

	CURRENT PERIOD		YEAR TO DATE-2 MONTHS	
	AMOUNT	%	AMOUNT	%
REVENUES:				
Revenue Remodeling	$ 70,252.37	62.09	$ 204,691.87	81.16
Revenue Comm. Remodeling	28,424.00	25.12	28,424.00	11.27
Revenue Ins. Remodeling	12,111.15	10.70	14,433.15	5.72
Miscellaneous	0.00	0.00	8.66	0.00
Revenue Building	2,296.00	2.03	4,592.50	1.82
Interest Income	68.46	0.06	68.46	0.03
TOTAL REVENUES	**113,151.98**	**100.00**	**252,218.64**	**100.00**
COST OF GOODS SOLD/JOB COSTS				
Direct Labor Comm. Remodel	2,966.51	2.62	5,678.51	2.25
Direct Labor Ins. Remodeling	96.00	0.08	117.00	0.05
Direct Labor Remodeling	6,294.51	5.56	11,208.39	4.44
Fringe Benefits Life/Health	41.95	0.04	83.90	0.03
Fringe Benefits Holiday	0.00	0.00	464.00	0.18
Fringe Benefits Vacation	360.00	0.32	3560.00	1.41
Emplr. Contr. FICA Expense	$ 1,836.84	1.62	3,618.92	1.44
Emplr. Contr. Workers Comp.	3,321.00	2.93	3,321.00	1.32
TOTAL LABOR	**$ 14,916.81**	**13.17**	**28,051.72**	**11.12**
Sub. Cont. Remodeling	35,728.41	31.58	81,099.27	32.15
Sub Cont. Com Remodeling	5,382.00	4.76	26,839.94	10.64
Sub Cont. Ins. Remodeling	870.00	0.77	870.00	0.34
TOTAL SUBCONTRACTOR	**$ 41,980.41**	**37.10**	**108,809.21**	**43.14**
Material Remodeling	19,334.67	17.09	31,793.84	12.61
Material Comm. Remodeling	243.89	0.22	6,005.53	2.38
Material Ins. Remodeling	261.23	0.23	491.76	0.19
Equipment Rental Comm.	240.00	0.21	240.00	0.10
Permits & Plans Remodeling	1,466.10	1.30	2,148.73	0.85
Dumping Fees Remodeling	1,100.00	0.97	1,250.00	0.50
Dumping Fees Commercial	303.75	0.27	303.75	0.12
Discounts Taken	-475.14	-0.42	-475.14	-0.19
TOTAL MATERIALS	**$ 22,474.50**	**19.87**	**41,758.47**	**16.56**
TOTAL COST GOODS SOLD	**$ 79,371.72**	**70.14**	**178,619.40**	**70.82**
GROSS PROFIT	**$ 33,780.26**	**29.86**	**73,599.24**	**29.18**
GENERAL & ADMIN. EXPENSES:				
Salary Officers	$ 8,006.85	7.08	16,249.05	6.44
Salary Office	2,814.75	2.49	5,504.50	2.18
Salary Supervisor	3,230.76	2.86	6,461.52	2.56

	CURRENT PERIOD		YEAR TO DATE-2 MONTHS	
	AMOUNT	%	AMOUNT	%
Service Work Orders/Warranty	355.98	0.31	900.93	0.36
Fringe Benefits Life/Health	401.17	0.35	802.34	0.32
Trash P/up (Dumpster)	53.80	0.05	107.60	0.04
Mobile Phone	152.59	0.13	303.22	0.12
Mobile Comm/Pager	69.78	0.06	136.69	0.05
Radio/Air Time	120.31	0.11	432.00	0.17
Telephone	340.50	0.30	661.76	0.26
Utilities	935.05	0.83	1,649.56	0.65
Business Meet. Misc.	46.00	0.04	173.56	0.07
Business Meet Principals	0.00	0.00	1,658.87	0.66
Bus. Meet. Travel	754.00	0.67	3,143.00	1.25
Business Gifts	0.00	0.00	202.50	0.08
Education	782.50	0.69	2,114.29	0.84
Office Supplies	370.14	0.33	733.79	0.29
Office Equipment	273.42	0.24	687.22	0.27
Computer Software Upgrades	0.00	0.00	496.80	0.20
Small Hand Tools <500	300.00	0.27	885.09	0.35
Safety supplies	0.00	0.00	30.07	0.01
Ref. Material & Data Manuals	0.00	0.00	34.95	0.01
Depreciation Expense	545.67	0.48	1,091.34	0.43
Accounting	380.00	0.34	760.00	0.30
Legal	686.50	0.61	686.50	0.27
Advertising	4,370.00	3.86	6,079.73	2.41
Postage	298.15	0.26	25.84	0.01
Dues & Subscription	0.00	0.00	55.00	0.02
Service Charges	41.24	0.04	41.24	0.02
Vehicle Costs	1,462.28	1.29	3,067.28	1.22
Taxes & License	196.00	0.17	196.00	0.08
Liability Insurance	3,607.00	3.19	3,607.00	1.43
Building Maint Misc.	0.00	0.00	146.21	0.06
Build. Repairs/Remodel	75.00	0.07	170.48	0.07
Bldg. Cleaning	260.00	0.23	390.00	0.15
Bldg. Supplies	0.00	0.00	37.27	0.01
Relocation Costs	371.34	0.33	439.68	0.17
TOTAL GEN & ADMIN EXPENSES	31,300.78	27.68	60,162.88	23.83
TOTAL OPERATING EXPENSES	35,701.57	31.55	65,651.48	26.03
OTHER EXPENSE:				
Interest Expense	1,703.90	1.51	3,384.43	1.34
TOTAL OTHER EXPENSE	**1,703.90**	**1.51**	**3,384.43**	**1.34**
NET PROFIT	**775.58**	**0.69**	**10,051.93**	**3.99**

Reading & Analyzing Your P & L

Let's say someone hands you your Profit & Loss statement for the first two months of the year. (For instance, look at the sample. Follow the steps below to review the first column which represents the most recent month and compare that to the year-to-date column which represents the past two months including the most recent month.) Here are the steps you would take in reviewing it:

1. Go ahead and look at the bottom line (dollars and percent) and see how you are doing!

2. Check the income/revenue line and see how that looks for the time period. Are you on target for the volume you wanted to achieve?

3. Check the percentage of job costs to see if that is in line with your markup. For instance, according to the markup chart later in this chapter, if you markup 50%, you are looking for a 67% job cost and a 33% gross profit. If you markup 40%, you can expect a gross profit of 28 1/2% and job costs of 61 1/2%. Your actual job cost percentage should be within 2% of your targeted number.

4. Check the percentage overhead is running to see how that fits your expectations/goals.

5. If all is well, and you show a positive net profit in line with your expectations pat yourself on the back and move on.

6. If one of the numbers—profit, income, job costs, overhead—is out of line, analyze the underlying numbers you have to support that information. Then get involved in preventing future overruns. What possibilities are there?

Be sure to call on your team for help in creating an action plan to bring the targeted volume or costs back into line. Then your P & L's over the next few months will tell you how effective your actions were in correcting the problem.

As you can see, analyzing a P & L involves **comparing company results to expectations.** Those expectations are best contained in your budget (see chapter 8).

What Should Be in the Job Cost Category?

You go to lunch with a friendly local remodeler. You and she decide to share information on your markups. Proudly you confide that you've achieved a 60% markup on costs. Then she tells you she marks up her jobs 80%! You find this unbelievable and you decide you'll each figure out your selling price for the same sample job. You start with exactly the same figures for labor hourly rates, subs and materials. Then you both figure out your selling price to the customer. You smugly feel your price will be much lower. You are astonished to discover that your selling prices are the same! How can this be when your markups are so different?

This scenario happens all the time. While all remodelers agree that job costs should include labor, subcontractors and materials, some remodelers include additional costs above those items. Every item taken out of overhead and moved to job costs increases job costs and reduces the markup percentage needed to reach the same selling price. In the above example, you obviously include more items in your definition of job costs than does your fellow remodeler. For that reason, your sales price is the same even though your markup is lower.

Case Study

SOLVING A MARKUP MYSTERY

Two remodelers—Jim and Mary—look at the same job. They return to the owner with the same sales price of $72,000. Their labor, material and sub costs are the same but because Jim puts some costs in overhead (marked with an asterisk) and Mary puts those same costs in job costs, they have different markups of 60% for Jim and 32% for Mary:

	JIM	MARY
LABOR	$15,000	$15,000
MATERIAL	15,000	15,000
SUBS	15,000	15,000
LABOR BURDEN*		4,500
LABOR BENEFITS*		2,500
PROD. MANAGER*		3,000
TOTAL JOB COSTS	$45,000	$55,000
MARKUP	X 1.6	X 1.32
SALES PRICE	$72,000	$72,000

All remodelers agree that job costs (cost of goods sold) should include:

- Labor
- Materials
- Subs

In addition to labor, materials and subs, your estimated job costs could include any or all of these:

- production manager salary (even if this is you, the owner)*
- labor burden including workers compensation, your social security contribution, federal and state unemployment for the field personnel*
- labor benefits like vacation, holidays, health insurance for the field personnel*
- vehicle costs for the field
- tools and equipment
- design costs
- sales commissions

BLINDSIDED BY BURDEN!

Recently a remodeler called about some financial problems he was having. I asked questions about his operation and found that he was relatively financially savvy. He defined his job costs as simply the labor (no burden), material and subs needed to do the job. All of the optional job cost areas, he covered in his overhead. As we discussed his company, he told me that he had discovered a wonderful market niche which provided a great deal of work because—for some reason—he was able to compete successfully on price.

For the past six months he had been working as a framing contractor for new home builders, selling only labor. A red flag went up in my mind. From experience, I knew that if he was selling labor and hadn't anticipated this change at the beginning of the year when he set up his workers comp insurance, and if he was not including the insurance and his other payroll related costs (employer's social security contribution, federal and state unemployment) as job costs by multiplying each project's labor by his burden percentage, he was in trouble. No wonder he was less expensive. His builder clients were not paying their full labor burden. This remodeler would be hit with a massive workers comp bill after his audit! And he would find that the other payroll-related expenses would eat up all of his markup and make these jobs losing jobs.

The easiest and surest way of assuring that each job pays its correct share of burden—whether it's a heavy-labor job or a light-labor job is to include burden in your estimates as a percentage of your labor. Figure out what your workers comp + employers contribution to social security + state and federal unemployment add up to. In a state where workers comp is 10% on labor, the percentage is likely to be 25-30%. Then you have an easy multiplier to use in creating a line item for burden in each of your estimates.

Consider putting all the costs that have an asterisk by them in job costs (and in your estimates as a line item, and in your budget as a job cost and in your actual job cost reports as a line item.) The most important principle here is that your company must decide on one definition of job costs, and that definition should be consistently adhered to in all reports.

Relationship Between Markup and Gross Profit

Many remodelers are unaware that their P & L is giving them direct feedback on how they are doing in achieving their markup. That's because there is a direct relationship between markup and your anticipated gross profit and job cost percentage. Just be sure your estimated "job costs" and your P & L "job costs" include exactly the same categories.

The area between the lines on the chart is considered the professional level of markup. You can still be a professional remodeler and mark up less, but usually the overhead costs inherent in paying yourself and your employees market rate and in running a first class operation push you into that level.

TO ACHIEVE THIS GROSS PROFIT	MARK UP COST BY THIS PERCENTAGE	JOB COST EXPECTED TO RUN
25.0	33.3	75%*
26.0	35.0	
27.0	37.0	
28.0	39.0	
28.5	40.0	
29.0	40.9	
30.0	43.0	
31.0	45.0	
32.0	47.0	
33.0	49.0	
33.5	50.0	66.5%
34.0	51.0	
35.0	54.0	
36.0	56.0	**PROFESSIONAL**
37.5	60.0	**LEVEL OF**
38.0	61.0	**OPERATION**
39.0	64.0	
40.0	66.7	60.0%
42.6	75.0	
45.0	82.0	
50.0	100.0	
66.7	200.0	
75.0	300.0	25%

* To fill in the Job Cost column, simply subtract Gross Profit from 100% (100% − 25%=75%)

Normally, you start with the gross profit you've determined will cover overhead and net profit and then figure out what markup will give you that percent of gross profit.

Let's take some examples:

If you need a 35% gross profit to cover 24% overhead and 11% net profit (and thus a 65% job cost), you will need to markup 54%, or

If you want to cover your 28% overhead and still make a 9% net profit (37% gross profit), you will need to markup approximately 60%.

Simple Conversion Math

The markup chart does some math for you but here are the formulae to do your own math:

1. **If you know the markup percent and want to determine the targeted gross profit percent, divide the markup percent by 1 plus the markup percent.**

   EXAMPLE: You are marking up 50% and want to know what gross profit percent that markup should achieve:

   $$50\% \text{ markup} = \frac{.50}{1 + .50} = .33 = 33\% \text{ gross profit}$$

2. **If you know the gross profit percent you need and want to determine the markup percent that will produce that gross profit, subtract the gross profit percent (expressed as a decimal) from 1, and divide that number into 1.**

   EXAMPLE: You have done your budget and know you must target a 37% gross profit (.37). You want to know what markup will achieve this gross profit.

   $$1 - .37 = .63 \qquad \frac{1}{.63} = 1.59 = 59\% \text{ markup}$$

Maximizing the Value of Your P & L Report

Here are some quick guidelines:

- Remember, the P & L Report is a management document for your use. Be sure it's formatted so you can understand it and use the valuable information it contains.

- Get comfortable with your P & L. It is like a job cost report (see later chapter on job costing)—but for the whole company. Know it well enough to be able to explain it to another person.

- Insist that you receive your reports within two weeks of the month end. Two weeks is a reasonable amount of time for the bookkeeper to prepare the report and yet it gives you timely information.

- Be sure to include percentages in a right hand column for ease of reading. These percentages are what you should be focusing on as you scan your report.

- Be sure the expense divisions are properly sorted. In particular, be sure that only items included in your job estimates as job costs are included in your P & L as job costs.

- Be sure to include labor burden and benefits in job costs so that both light labor and heavy labor jobs are accurately priced and so that you won't get caught holding the bag in your workers comp audit.

- Zero in on the projected job cost percentage based on your markup. For instance if you markup 50%, you are anticipating a 33% gross profit and 67% job cost. Job costs that run too high are the most common problem area for remodelers. Be aggressive about solving it!

■ Watch that all of your individual job cost reports totalled together equal your job costs on your P & L statement.

■ Always put your owner's salary in your P & L as a cost of doing business. You might sort your salary into job costs if you work on the job or if you are production manager and that is considered a job cost in your company. Or you may put your owner's salary in overhead if you sell or administer. Do not take your base salary from the bottom line net profit.

■ Be sure to include depreciation (on equipment, vehicles, etc.) in your P & L as a line item overhead expense each month. Ask your accountant how much it should be. Since your end-of-year report will contain this, you should get accustomed to seeing it as a reduction of your normal monthly report.

■ If you have two diversified types of businesses (perhaps custom home building and remodeling or replacement windows and design/build remodeling) keep income and expense separated for each branch of your company (even though you keep them on the same P & L report.) That way you can analyze income, job costs, gross profit for each segment separately and make informed decisions as to whether to grow, maintain or reduce certain parts of your business.

■ One of the most valuable analyses of your P & L is to compare it to the budget for the time period (see chapter 8 on Budgeting). Your budget creates a roadmap to profit and your P & L shows how you are doing in staying on that roadmap. By analyzing this monthly, you are able to take quick action when you see the company going off track in some area.

This chapter has focused on the first critical financial report that you will need to maximize profits for the company. Your P & L is your good friend that delivers straightforward information on where your company stands. It also gives you important clues as to where you can do better.

CHAPTER THREE CHECK-UP

1. Using the Markup Chart

It's the beginning of the year and you are checking whether your current markup is enough to cover your budgeted overhead. Figure out these problems by using the markup chart on page 31:

   a. Your overhead is 25% and you want a 5% net profit, what do you have to markup?

   b. In the problem above, what are you expecting your job costs to run?

   c. You are currently marking up 45%, what should your gross profit be?

   d. What should your job costs be in item C?

   e. What two major categories are covered by gross profit?

2. The first category of costs subtracted from your income in a Profit and Loss Report is _____.

3. The category of costs that includes postage, rent, office salaries is _____.

4. If the net profit number is in parentheses, it is a

_____

5. The job cost percentage on your P & L report should match up with the job costs targeted by the _____ that you apply when you estimate a job.

6. Company owners should pay themselves from the net profit of the company.

☐ True   ☐ False

CHECK YOUR ANSWERS BELOW

ANSWERS

1. Using the Markup Chart

    a. 43%   b. 70%

    c. 31%   d. 69%

    e. Overhead and net profit are the two major categories covered by gross profit.

2. The first category of costs subtracted from your income in a Profit and Loss Report is Job Costs or Cost of Sales.

3. The category of costs that includes postage, rent, office salaries is Overhead or General and Administrative Expenses (G & A).

4. If the net profit number is in parentheses, it is a loss.

5. The job cost percentage should match up with the job costs targeted by the markup that you apply when you estimate a job.

6. False. The company owner's salary is a cost of doing business and should be included as part of job costs or overhead—or both.

Chapter 4

Method of Accounting

*"Money is a terrible master but
an excellent servant."*

P.T. Barnum

In order to read and make sense of your P & L, begin by asking what method of accounting was used to produce it. That's because there are a number of ways to report your revenue (income) and your costs (expenses). Each accounting method differs in its answer to the question "When is a sale a sale?" The method of accounting that you use makes a big difference in how valuable the reports will be to you in managing your company. Let's look at four methods for producing your P & L report:

- Cash
- Billing
- Completed Jobs
- Percentage of Completion

THE CASH METHOD:

Question: "When is a sale a sale?"
Answer: "When we actually get the money!"

In the cash method, **income includes all revenues actually received** and **expense includes all bills actually paid.** We must have actually collected the money for it to be income. We must have actually paid the bill for it to be an expense.

This method gives you a good idea of cash flow for the time period. However, this report potentially can be very misleading. Collect a first draw, and it goes to income. But you haven't earned that money. You haven't done the work it pays for—you've just gotten an advance. Behind on paying your bills? Can't pay $20,000 to the lumber yard that you owe? It won't show under expense because with the cash method you only show the bills you've actually paid.

Most entrepreneurs including remodelers use the cash method at first. Get out of it as fast as you can! Even the IRS (for different reasons) wants you out of the cash basis.

IRS MAY MAKE YOU DROP CASH BASIS OF ACCOUNTING

A late 1995 report from C.W. Amos & Company, Certified Public Accountants and Business Consultants in Annapolis and Baltimore, MD, noted that recent court decisions and IRS rulings are frowning on use of the cash basis for tax purposes. "Contractors should consider whether a voluntary change in accounting method to the accrual basis would be in their best interest," notes the report. "It seems that absent congressional action, the IRS is determined to place all contractors, large and small, on the accrual basis." You'll want to check with your accountant as to IRS policy at the time you read this book.

Accrual methods of accounting recognize income and expense when they are earned and incurred without concern as to when the money actually changes hands. In an accrual method all invoices are entered as expenses when they are received. Thus your job costs are more up-to-date. Knowing a P & L is produced on an accrual basis only tells you it is not on a cash basis. You need to know which type of accrual.

THE BILLINGS ACCRUAL METHOD:

Question: "When is a sale a sale?"
Answer: "As soon as we bill the money!"

In the billings method, **income includes all billed receivables (money people owe you) and expenses include all billed payables (money you owe someone else).**

This method, too, can be a very misleading way to present company operations. One of our business management rules for remodelers is to stay ahead of your client in your billings and collections. But that "staying ahead" means many of your reports would look too rosy. Others might look too dire.

For instance, you may have actually completed 30% of a job, yet billed the owner 45%. Because this method recognizes all billed amounts as income, your P & L report will show that 45% as income against only 30% of the job costs. Your next reports, however, will show 55% of the billings against 70% of the job costs. In this circumstance, your P & L's would at first show your financial position as much rosier than reality. Then your later P & L's would show a poor picture as though your job costs were running very high in comparison to your income. You want to manage with realistic figures.

The Completed Jobs Accrual Method:

Question: "When is a sale a sale?"
Answer   "Why, it's not a sale until the job is finished (or substantially finished)."

This method tallies all money coming in for a job and all money paid and billed for the costs on the job but **does not show these as income and expense on the P & L until the job is completed. Meanwhile overhead expenses are usually shown as they are expended each month.**

Because this method is the slowest to show new dollars in income, it may well be chosen by your accountant to present information for tax purposes since it may defer your income to the next year for tax purposes. Of course, ultimately that income catches up with you in the next year. If you use this method for your management reports, your profit and loss statement may look too negative.

If you are a specialty contractor and your jobs are very short in duration (under a week), you can use this method effectively. However for full line remodelers, this method is the **most misleading**. Many accountants will recommend that you use the completed jobs method because it is the recommended method for new home builders. The accountant may not differentiate you as a remodeler.

However, do not use the completed jobs method of accounting for your management reports if your jobs are under construction for more than a week or two. Your day-to-day financials should be produced with the following method.

THE PERCENTAGE OF COMPLETION METHOD:

Question: "When is a sale a sale?"
Answer: "A sale happens when we have actually completed some percentage of the work."

With the percentage of completion accrual method, **income is figured on the basis of your sales price multiplied by the percent of the job which has actually been completed. Expenses are also figured on the basis of the amount of the work completed.** This method adds to your P & L gradually as you complete the job. By the time the job is done, all of the income and expenses and profit will be included. This method makes considerable sense because we can't count money as our own until we produce the product. We want to focus on money we've **earned** in our P & L and this method does just that.

This method can be used on jobs which extend across an accounting period. In other words, if the job is not fully completed at the time the report is done but you still want a realistic idea of where the company stands, use a consistent method for deciding how the percentage of completion will be assessed on a job (see box). Then if the Jones job is 38% complete at the end of June, 38% of its revised contract amount (including change orders) will be entered as income and 38% of updated and expected costs will be listed as expense.

Pros and Cons of Percentage of Completion

The percentage of completion method of accounting comes the closest to giving a realistic picture of how much money the company has earned in a time period vs.

the costs incurred to earn that amount of money. The main disadvantage to this method is being able to devise a consistent (and consistently applied) system for accurately estimating what percent of a job has been completed at the end of each month.

There is a secondary disadvantage. This report cannot be read as a cash flow statement. You may have earned $15,000 more on a job than you've collected. Your P & L may look rosy but the checking account may be low. Don't mistake profits and cash flow. As you will see in the Cash Flow chapter (chapter 7), a well run remodeling business should stay ahead of the client in collections. In that case, your cash flow position will stay rosier than your profit position.

Using percentage of completion is more work for your company each month. But the resulting increase in accuracy far outweighs these drawbacks.

When we study the Balance Sheet, we'll see some special entries caused by using this accounting method.

APPLYING THE PERCENTAGE OF COMPLETION METHOD

Here's how *Matt Davitt, Davitt Woodworks, Inc.*, applies the percentage of completion method to generate his P & L each month. He uses a computerized spreadsheet and by entering the numbers in columns 1,2,5, and 9, the other columns are automatically filled in by the computer program.

APPLYING THE PERCENTAGE OF COMPLETION METHOD (CONTINUED)

	1*	2*	3	4	5*	6	7	8	9*	10
Contract Name	Total Contract Price	Estimated Job Costs	Estimated Gross Profit	% Est Gross Profit	Actual Cost to Date	% of Compl.	Earned G/P	Actual Cost and GP	Total Amount Invested by Client	Unbilled Revenue OR (Unearned Revenue)
Harris	$325,582.	$231,549.	$94,033.	28.88%	$ 51,574.	22%	$20,687.	$72,261.	$120,000.	($47,739.)
Cary	250,000.	180,574.	69,426.	27.77%	156,230.	87%	60,401.	216,631.	184,268.	32,363.
Resner	89,525.	51,625.	37,900.	42.33%	45,138.	87%	32,973.	78,111.	59,791.	18,320.
Grogan	6,500.	3,450.	3,050.	46.92%	913.	26%	793.	1,706.	3,795.	(2,089.)

Total $855.

1. Total contract price or revised contract price by last change order.
2. Estimated direct cost from your estimate and change orders.
3. Estimated gross profit from your estimate and change orders, (col 1 – col 2)
4. Percentage you estimate for gross profit on the job, (col 3 divided by col 1)
5. What you have been invoiced to date from subs, vendors, etc. for that particular job.

* numbers must be entered. Other columns figured by spread sheet.

6. Percentage you have completed for that project . (col 5 divided by col 2) .
7. Actual gross profit you have earned. (col 3 x col 6)
8. Total of direct cost to date plus earned gross profit to date. (col 5 + col 7)
9. Amount you have invoiced the customer to date.
10. Journal entry to balance sheet and income statement to reflect actual numbers for the month.

Earned but Unbilled Revenue: Work performed but not yet invoiced will increase your sales for the month and also be an asset on balance sheet. (Positive number = Asset)

Billed but Unearned Revenue: Deposits or invoices for work not yet completed will reduce sales for the month and be a liability on your balance sheet. (Negative number = Liability)

Note: For current month's P & L, you have to isolate amount of work done in current month from that done in previous months!

Does Method of Accounting Make a Difference?

Let's take some simple financial information and try out the various methods. Remember they differ by their definition of when we treat a sale as income or when we treat incoming money as true income. You might want to test your knowledge by covering up the answers and working them out for yourself!

BALANCE ✓

Case Study

PROBLEM: Joe Smith runs a very small 1-job-at-a-time remodeling company. It's the end of the first quarter of the year. Joe began a $100,000 job ($70,000 in estimated job costs) on January 1 and by March 31, here is what has transpired—

Joe's job costs, for which he's received invoices are $35,000.

Joe has reviewed his job costs and they are right on target with his estimate.

He's paid $20,000 of those costs and has $15,000 still unpaid.

He's billed the owner $70,000 and has actually collected $60,000.

His low overhead has run only $10,000.

Those are the facts. What net profit would Joe have under each method of accounting?

ANSWER:

METHOD	CASH	BILLINGS	COMPLETED JOBS	% OF COMPLETION
INCOME	60,000	70,000	0	50,000*
JOB COSTS	20,000	35,000	0	35,000
GROSS PROFIT	40,000	35,000	0	15,000
OVERHEAD	10,000	10,000	10,000	10,000
NET PROFIT	30,000	25,000	(10,000)	5,000

Since job costs were on target (no anticipated overrun) and were 50% of the total estimated expended, we can antici- pate that earned income was 50% of total project sale.

Put yourself in Joe Smith's position. He wants to know just how his business did in the first quarter. He wants to know if he made money. Did you ever consider that legitimate accounting procedures might produce a "correct" (but sometimes mislead- ing) answer ranging from a $10,000 loss to a $30,000 profit—a $40,000 spread—given the same numbers?

Let's ask a more precise question on Joe's behalf. How much income did his business earn in the first quarter and what did it cost to produce that income? Joe's most accurate answer is pro- duced by the percentage of completion method which shows a net profit of $5000.

The percentage of completion method is the best way to match earned income against the expense incurred to earn that income. Thus it gives a remodeler the most accurate accounting of their current financial picture.

To avoid a very skewed picture of your business that would be overly optimistic or too pessimistic, work with your accountant to decide how to consistently determine the percentage of completion of each job at the end of each month.

CHAPTER FOUR CHECK-UP

1. Comparing Methods of Accounting

Ellen runs Ellen's Remodeling. It is the end of June—half way through the year. Her only job is a huge $300,000 mansion remodeling. Here are some facts:

- She estimated her costs on this job would be $200,000.

- She has been billed for $150,000 between all the labor, materials and subs.

- Ellen has paid 120,000 of those bills and has $30,000 left to pay.

- She figures that she has completed 75% of the job and that her original estimate is right on target.

- She has billed the owners for $175,000 and they have paid her $160,000.

- Her overhead has run $35,000.

- Ellen has been doing her P & L on a cash basis and wants to change to percentage of completion. Will that make a difference in her reports?

Figure it out using the following chart:

	Cash Basis	Percentage of Completion _____%
Income		
Job Costs		
Gross Profit		
Overhead		
Net Profit		

2. Only your accountant needs to understand your method of accounting.

a. True

b. False

3. The method of accounting that is most realistic for the full line remodeler is called _____. It is preferred because it shows only earned income as revenue and actual expenses incurred to earn that income as job costs.

CHECK YOUR ANSWERS ON THE NEXT PAGE → → →

ANSWERS

1.	Cash Basis	Percentage of Completion (75%)
Income	160,000	225,000
Job Costs	120,000	150,000
Gross Profit	40,000	75,000
Overhead	35,000	35,000
Net Profit	5,000	40,000

Ellen shows a much better result under percentage of completion because her collections from the owners trail job progress. Were she ahead of the clients in collections (as she should be), her cash basis picture would be rosier than percentage of completion. Percentage of completion shows most accurately what has truly been earned by the remodeler.

2. False. The method of accounting used for your reports is critical to you, the owner.

3. The method of accounting that is most realistic for the full line remodeler is Percentage of Completion.

Chapter 5

Your Balance Sheet

"Since the balance sheet portrays the financial health of a business, it is the main statement for analysis of solvency and liquidity, the prospect of business failure or slowness in meeting obligations."
Robert G. Finney,
Every Manager's Guide to Business Finance

ifteen years ago, I was one of those remodelers (maybe like you) who used to scoot by all the financial reports and go directly to the P & L to find out whether our company had made money. I was usually given a Balance Sheet as well, but I had no idea what it meant. The Balance Sheet didn't seem to be as dynamic or vital a report as the P & L which showed whether we had made any profit during the last month. Oh, how blind I was!

If you are giving the Balance Sheet minimal attention like I was, start valuing all the information that it contains to help you.

The Balance Sheet shows:

▪ The financial state of the company on a given day.

▪ What the company owns (assets) and who owns it (liabilities).

▪ How much debt the company is carrying.

▪ How much money the owner has in the company.

▪ How much money is owed the company (receivables).

▪ How much money the company owes on jobs and overhead (payables).

WHAT'S THE DIFFERENCE?

There's a huge difference between what the Balance Sheet represents and what your P & L represents. Let's say your company is seven years old. You get an end of year, December 31, Balance Sheet and P & L.

Your Balance sheet will show the results—the sum total—of your seven years of work. It will show how much of value your company has accumulated and how many loans you have and what your company is worth if you cashed out. It's the score sheet for all seven years.

Your P & L takes a snippet of time—a one year cut in this case—and shows how you ended the year based on beginning January with zero. The P & L may show a profit of $20,000 but your balance sheet may show that money being swallowed up in massive debt and your company's worth being negative.

If you compare these two reports to sports team reports, the P & L shows the results of the current game, the Balance Sheet shows the long term record.

What is a Balance Sheet?

The Balance Sheet is a snapshot showing the financial position of the business in a specific moment of time. It shows **Assets**—what the company has in cash, billings, and equipment, as well as who owns it. **Liabilities** show the ownership of others (your vendors, your bank) and **Equity** shows your ownership—or in a corporation, the ownership of stockholders.

This report is called a balance sheet because it does balance!

Here is the equation:

ASSETS = LIABILITIES + OWNER'S EQUITY

Another—and a simpler—way to explain the balance sheet is:

What the company has = what others own + what you own

You might object "but no one owns this company but me!" Liabilities (perhaps car loans, or loans on land, or bills from vendors) actually represent the amount of the company subject to the interest or ownership of others. Let's turn this equation around to look at the balance sheet from the point of view of equity (your ownership or the stockholder's ownership—and you likely own most the stock.)

OWNER'S EQUITY = ASSETS − LIABILITIES

Or in the simpler version:

What you own = what the company has - what others own or
have interest in

BALANCE SHEET

ASSETS

CURRENT ASSETS

Cash on hand	$100.00	
Checking	8,168.52	
Savings	70,134.31	
Accounts Receivable	41,461.59	
Employee Advances	200.00	
Due from Officer	47,567.53	
Prepaid Insurance	12,119.30	
Costs in Excess Billings	71,179.19	
Federal Estimated Taxes Paid	2,702.00	
State Estimated Taxes	2,000.00	
TOTAL CURRENT ASSETS		$239,295.40

PROPERTY, PLANT & EQUIPMENT

Equipment	$13,912.13	
Truck	24,474.04	
Less Accumulated Depreciation	(26,162.00)	
NET BOOK VALUE OF PROPERTY, PLANT & EQUIPMENT		12,224.17

OTHER ASSETS

TOTAL OTHER ASSETS		00.00

TOTAL ASSETS	$251,519.57

BALANCE SHEET (CONTINUED)

LIABILITIES AND EQUITY

CURRENT LIABILITIES

Accounts Payable	$63,810.53	
Billing in Excess of Cost	35,106.76	
FICA Taxes Payable	771.39	
Federal Taxes Payable	1,159.96	
State Taxes Payable	873.85	
City Tax Payable	341.67	
Note Payable	10,000.00	
Note Payable 1993 Vehicle	13,092.57	
TOTAL CURRENT LIABILITIES		$125,156.73

LONG-TERM DEBT

Loan from Shareholders	$00.00	
TOTAL LONG-TERM DEBT		00.00

STOCKHOLDERS' EQUITY

Common Stock	500.00	
Paid in Capital	4,500.00	
Retained Earnings	140,002.56	
Profit and Loss	18,639.72 −	
TOTAL STOCKHOLDERS' EQUITY		$126,362.84
TOTAL LIABILITIES AND STOCKHOLDERS' EQUITY		$251,519.57

The Three Balance Sheet Categories

Let's look at what the three main balance sheet categories represent and you'll see just how logical your balance sheet is. It's no harder to understand than that estimate for a porch enclosure!

Assets—what does the company have? This category includes anything of value whether it's paid for or not. Assets are listed in order of the speed with which you can convert them into cash.

   Current assets are cash or can become cash or can offset the need for cash within 1 year.

   Fixed assets are property of the company that usually will be owned for a long time like land, buildings, equipment. They are usually valued at the price paid and depreciation is shown on them (and subtracted from the price paid). Items under fixed assets are often difficult to assess for true value. For instance, goodwill may be carried here and what is that really worth? What is the office building really worth if we have to sell it quickly? These are difficult to judge.

Liabilities—who do you owe for the assets? Another way to look at this is, other than you the owner, who owns the assets? the bank? your family? You may not have considered your lumberyard or your bank as "owning" part of your company but—in a sense—they do!

   Current liabilities are obligations that must be paid within 12 months, like a short term bank note, or accounts payable to your vendors and subcontractors. Payments owed within the next year on your vehicles would be listed here but those after 1 year would be long term liabilities.

Long term liabilities are obligations which are not due for twelve months or more.

Net Worth or Owner's Equity—the value of the part of the company that you own. This is the excess of assets over liabilities. In a sense, you get the leftovers. What isn't owed to others is owned by you. In a partnership there would be an account for each partner. In a corporation, this would be Stockholders' Equity.

Under this section will be **Retained Earnings,** the total amount of net income retained over time for use by the business. If this is negative, then the business has been losing money (or conceivably has paid out more in dividends than it has earned).

Once you understand how a Balance Sheet is "built," it's easy to see why the value of what the company has must equal the value of what is owed to or owned by others. Now that we understand how to "read" the Balance Sheet, let's look at what we can do with some of our Balance Sheet information.

FIGURE WORKING CAPITAL

Subtracting current liabilities from current assets gives you working capital—a measure of your capacity for business expansion and growth.

CURRENT ASSETS – CURRENT LIABILITIES = WORKING CAPITAL

Working capital in our sample Balance Sheet is:

$239,295 – $125,156 = $114,139

Ratios

A ratio is a set of numbers showing the relationship between two similiar things. Those numbers are expressed this way—8:3. Perhaps this ratio expresses the number of healthful calories that Gerry eats compared to the number of unhealthful calories. The ratio tells us that for every 8 healthful calories she eats, she is eating 3 unhealthy ones. The ratios we will develop will show our financial health.

Much of the information we want to know about our financial health comes from ratios which are developed from line items in the Balance Sheet. Only one percent of remodelers understand and use ratios and yet they are quick and easy to apply once your reports are in order. They'll give you some very valuable information. Here are four of the most important ratios for remodelers.

☐ Current Ratio

☐ Acid Test or Quick Ratio

☐ Debt to Equity Ratio

☐ Return on Equity Ratio

$$\text{CURRENT RATIO} = \frac{\text{CURRENT ASSETS}}{\text{CURRENT LIABILITIES}} = ? : 1$$

This is the most popular measure of solvency. It shows the relationship of a dollar in current assets to a dollar in current liabilities. From this division you will get the first number of the ratio and that will be compared to 1. These numbers actually represent dollars as you'll see in the example below.

The larger the first number, the better the company position. There is little agreement on what this ratio should be for a remodeler but close to 2 (2:1) is probably ideal. This means the company has $2 in current assets for every $1 in current liabilities. **This is a measure of short term ability to pay debt.** Less than a .75 : 1 ratio (75¢ in current assets to every $1 in current liabilities), and there is a shortage of working capital. More than 2, you may not be using your available resources well. You may be overcapitalized and should invest in outside investments that have a good return.

The current ratio for the sample Balance Sheet on page 54 is:

$$\frac{\$239,295}{\$125,156} = 1.9 = 1.9 : 1$$

This means that the company has $1.90 in current assets for every $1 in current liabilities. They could pay off all of their short term debt quickly and still have some money left over.

$$\text{ACID TEST OR QUICK RATIO} = \frac{\text{CASH + RECEIVABLES}}{\text{CURRENT LIABILITIES}} = ? : 1$$

This Quick Ratio is an even stronger **measure of firm's abilities to pay current liabilities** because it uses cash and receivables only, instead of all current assets as the current ratio did. The acceptable range is 1.0–2.0 (you have $1–2 in cash + receivables for every $1 in current liabilities).

If your Quick Ratio is below this range, you are undercapitalized (have too little money invested in your company). If it's over 2.0, you might be over-capitalized (have too much money at risk in your company) and may want to invest extra funds in outside investments.

The Quick Ratio in our sample is:

$$\frac{\$62,066 + \$41,461}{\$125,156} = \frac{\$103,527}{\$125,156} = .83$$

The $62,066 includes cash plus checking plus savings since they are all cash. The Quick Ratio would be expressed as .83 : 1. The company has .83 cents in prime current assets for every $1 in current liabilities.

$$\text{DEBT TO EQUITY RATIO} = \frac{\text{TOTAL LIABILITIES}}{\text{NET WORTH/ OWNER'S EQUITY}} = \ ? : 1$$

This ratio is a measure of the **level of the company's debt load.** Another way to look at this is the amount of assets provided by your creditors for each dollar of assets provided by you, the owner. The smaller the number (the less the creditor-provided assets) the better. A good ratio for remodeling is .9 – 2.0, or .90 cents to $2 in creditor-provided assets for every $1 you provided.

The Debt to Equity Ratio in our sample Balance Sheet is:

$$\frac{\$125,156}{\$126,362} = .99$$

Thus creditors are providing .99 for every $1 the owner or shareholders are providing for company use, right in the correct range.

$$\text{RETURN ON EQUITY} = \frac{\text{NET INCOME BEFORE TAXES (FROM P \& L)}}{\text{NET WORTH/OWNER'S EQUITY}}$$

This ratio is a measure of the return on the owner's investment. The higher the percentage, the better. The higher the risk taken in your business, the higher this return should be. All small businesses are high risk. Remodelers need to consider what return they could receive on their money in other investments and look at this return with great scrutiny. If you could receive 7% return on a safe Treasury bond, then compare this with the return from your business which is inherently risky. Note that we are not talking about your salary here—only the net profit.

The Balance Sheet and Percentage of Completion Accounting

On the sample Balance Sheet you'll notice a line item under current assets called "Costs in Excess of Billings." This tells us the company is using percentage of completion method for accounting. This line contains any job cost billings or payments that could not be put on the P & L because they represented the excess over the percentage of completion decided upon on that job. If the P & L contained 38% of the Harris jobs costs but there were additional costs incurred over that (in excess), they would be held here in the balance sheet.

You'll also see an entry under Liabilities for "Billings in Excess of Cost" which contains the additional billings to the consumer which could not be supported by the job completion percentage used in the P & L.

Start valuing your Balance Sheet as more than a "dust cover" for your P & L. It gives you some unique information. In fact, this document is what your bank, your lender, your bonding agency want to see. Why? Because they know it is the best representation of your company's **true worth.** By using ratios over a period of years you will also have some critical measures that will help you progress to a healthier and richer company.

CHAPTER FIVE CHECK-UP

1. Here are lots of financial categories and numbers. Create a simple Balance Sheet and Profit and Loss statement in the boxes below:

a. Total liabilities	$50,000
b. Overhead	120,000
c. Owner's equity	50,000
d. Current assets	45,000
e. Income	500,000
f. Current liability	30,000
g. Net profit	40,000
h. Long term liability	20,000
i. Total assets	100,000
j. Job costs	340,000
k. Fixed assets	55,000
l. Gross profit	160,000

BALANCE SHEET

```
┌─────────────────────────────────────────────────────────┐
│                         P & L                             │
│ ──────────────────────────────────    ─────────────────── │
│                                                           │
│ ──────────────────────────────────    ─────────────────── │
│                                                           │
│ ──────────────────────────────────    ─────────────────── │
│                                                           │
│ ──────────────────────────────────    ─────────────────── │
│                                                           │
│ ──────────────────────────────────    ─────────────────── │
└─────────────────────────────────────────────────────────┘
```

2. The Balance Sheet always balances.

☐ True   ☐ False

3. The Balance Sheet shows your company's financial position on the day on which it is prepared.

☐ True   ☐ False

4. The three major categories the balance sheet is divided into are:

a. _____

b. _____

c. _____

5. Current Liabilities must be paid within _____.

6. To get the current ratio, divide _____ by _____. This shows how solvent the company is.

CHECK YOUR ANSWERS ON THE NEXT PAGE → → →

ANSWERS

1.

BALANCE SHEET	
d. Current assets	$45,000
k. Fixed assets	55,000
i. Total assets	100,000
f. Current liabilities	30,000
h. Long term liabilities	20,000
a. Total liabilities	50,000
c. Owner's equity	50,000

PROFIT & LOSS STATEMENT	
e. Income	$500,000
j. Job costs	340,000
l. Gross Profit	160,000
b. Overhead	120,000
g. Net Profit	40,000

2. True. The value of the Assets must equal Liabilities plus Net Worth/Equity.

3. True. The Balance Sheet is a snapshot of the company's financial position on the day on which the report is prepared.

4. The Balance Sheet categories are Assets, Liabilities, and Net Worth or Equity.

5. Current Liabilities must be paid within one year.

6. To get the current ratio, divide the current assets by the current liabilities. This ratio shows just how solvent the company is.

Chapter 6

Accurate Job Costing

"Every business has two financial objectives:
One is to make money; the other, more elusive, is
to make money consistently."
Dave Linigerr, founder of RE/MAX, a nationwide realty firm

 make money consistently in remodeling, you need accurate estimating. In order to have accurate estimating, you need accurate job costing to give you constant feedback on your estimating system.

As you prepare a project estimate, you are setting many goals. Your goals are the material cost you hope to meet or beat, the labor cost you hope to achieve and the subcontractor cost you anticipate.

Once you have sold the job and production begins, you keep records of your expenses for that job in each category of your estimate. How are you doing on meeting these goals? This collection of data is critical to your success, because it sets the stage for accuracy in your future estimates. Only by gathering accurate and timely job cost information will you be able to gauge job performance and keep your estimating information up-to-date.

Job costing has a second important benefit—as a big picture financial control. You are working hard to keep total job costs at the percentage of income you target with your markup. You watch your P & L to see how you are doing overall. You watch each individual job to insure that the job is staying on target. If you need to lower job costs, it is much easier, at the individual job level, to investigate the overrun problem and solve it.

Eroding Job Costs

Reviewing Profit and Loss statements shows clearly that job costs are usually a remodeler's single biggest area of expenditure—often running 65-70% (or more) of total company expenditures. If they run out of control, your business is out of control. If your job costs are 79% but were planned for 70%, you will lose 9% from the net profit line. Thus job costs need careful analysis. In a remodeling company where expenses are out of control, the greatest problem often lies with job costs that are overrunning estimates by a significant margin and bleeding the company of profitability.

Accurate job costing data is needed for three reasons:

■ to help tighten cost control on ongoing jobs

■ to prevent overruns on future jobs

■ to build a cost history for estimating

COLLECTING JOB COST DATA HELPS TIGHTEN YOUR CURRENT JOB EXPENDITURES. Knowing that an ongoing job is beginning to overrun can help you tighten up on costs on that job. You may be able to recoup some of your costs through better monitored change orders, by using different subs, or by encouraging workers to produce more efficiently. Thus it is helpful to have job cost reports on a weekly or biweekly basis to rein-in overruns on current jobs before they get out-of-hand and you end up losing money on the job. By reviewing cost data with your salespeople and your production manager and lead carpenter, you are sending a clear signal that jobs must generate the gross profit the company needs to operate. Jobs only generate that gross profit by coming in on budget.

JOB COST DATA PREVENTS FUTURE OVERRUNS. The single most powerful reason for obtaining accurate job costs is to produce data that can be analyzed to prevent future overruns. Many companies, when they first start getting job cost data or before their books are computerized, produce job costs only at the end of each job. However, simply knowing that your actual costs are showing a trend to exceed the estimated costs does not tell you whether the problem is in:

- inaccurate estimating

- inefficient job productivity

- a combination of both

This assessment needs to come from careful analysis of the data contained in the job cost. I like to call this analysis an "autopsy." To do an accurate "autopsy," assemble the salesperson, estimator, production manager and lead carpenter—in a small company, these may all be you—and try to find **what** (not who) caused the job to overrun. For larger companies the most likely culprits are a messy handoff between sales and production or inadequate blueprints and specifications. Remember, this is a team effort to help the company avoid future problems.

JOB COST DATA HELPS YOU BUILD A HISTORY OF COSTS. Many remodelers use detailed job costing from previous jobs to help them price out prospective jobs. If the Kerrigans want a kitchen bumpout and screened porch on their two story brick colonial, you can use the costs on previous similiar jobs to generate a quick ballpark price and then again later to develop a tight bid for doing the Kerrigan project. Past projects act as an accurate cost reference for new work.

Collecting Accurate Job Cost Data

Early in this book, we talked about how simple the remodeler's questions are, but how much work is needed to assemble the answers. Your question here is "Are my jobs coming in as estimated?" The data needed to give you that answer is fairly voluminous.

For accurate job costing start with three ingredients:

1. an estimate cover sheet that summarizes your cost categories. This information is entered into the system and actual costs are tracked for those same categories.

2. prompt and accurately filled out time cards.

3. invoices from suppliers and subs with job names or numbers. (Ask your personnel and your suppliers to use one sales ticket per job. That saves you the extra work of chasing down which piece of material went to which job.)

Purchase Orders (P.O.'s) Can Help Job Costing

Purchase orders are a paperwork system in which you use a multicopy form to write out the material you are ordering, where it is to be ordered from, and the price with any delivery or extra expense. Using purchase orders—while adding another bureaucratic level to your buying—saves time and effort for the larger remodeler by:

1. fixing the price, specifications and delivery information for everyone involved in buying, using or accounting for the materials used on a job.

2. allowing the estimator or production manager to price the materials one time. Otherwise materials must be priced in estimating, in purchasing and in reviewing job tickets.

3. allowing the bookkeeper to check the invoice against P.O., reducing the need for management to get involved.

4. letting the company bookkeeper know what purchase invoices are outstanding.

You can choose between simpler or more complex levels of job cost tracking. The low volume remodeler may collect data only in the labor, subs and material estimating classifications. The more sophisticated remodeler often breaks down carpentry areas into smaller segments like roof framing, roof sheathing, setting windows and doors, job cleanup, and may use 16-25 classifications. While this is very valuable information, it creates considerable extra work for the field, the production manager and the bookkeeper. Do not collect data in that detail unless you intend to analyze it carefully and reap the benefits in improved job cost analysis.

MANUAL JOB COST REPORT

This is an example of a very simple manually prepared job cost report with a minimum of categories tracked. As you can see, this remodeler has considerable work to do to bring estimates and actual costs into line.

	ESTIMATE	ACTUAL	VARIANCE
Labor	$ 720.00	$1,886.55	($1,166.55)
Plumbing	1,825.00	1,825.00	0.00
Millwork	0.00	345.68	(345.68)
Lumber	150.00	493.94	(343.94)
Electrical	290.00	260.00	30.00
Insulation	75.00	57.15	17.85
Drywall	530.00	488.35	41.65
Ceramic	1,260.00	1,200.00	60.00
Hardware	535.00	661.78	(126.78)
Misc.	150.00	258.25	(108.25)
	$ 5,535.00	**$ 7,476.70**	**(1,941.70)**

Manual vs. Computerized Job Costs

Job costs can be accurately assembled in either a manual or a computerized system. When done manually, they are extremely laborious to generate and often just don't get done. One of the major benefits of computerizing your accounting (that rarely gets mentioned) is the ease and frequency with which job cost reports can be published. That's because the data is already being entered for other purposes and then is used (in an integrated system) for costing. Extra labor is required only to enter estimate summaries in the categories against which the costs will be compared. So if you are planning to buy accounting software be sure you ask about the ease with which data can be transferred into job costs. Then you can have your job cost data hourly if you wish!

COMPUTER GENERATED JOB COST REPORT

This is one remodeler's computer generated summary cover page. There are more finely detailed reports with all the backup information that can also be printed if the remodeler wants to find out what payments went into a category.

SAMPLE: COMPUTER GENERATED JOB COST REPORT

Job #95161   JOB BUDGET STATUS REPORT   by: J.J.
Simmons Job   DIRECT COSTS   08/28/95

Cost Category	Cost Category Descriptions	Budget	Paid to Date	Accrued Costs to Date	Budget Balance
110	Planning	200.00	84.00	84.00	116.00
200	Demo	0.00	87.74	88.00	(88.00)
210	Tear Out	260.00	140.00	140.00	120.00
520	Masonry	580.00	450.00	450.00	130.00
700	Wood Framing	2940.00	1344.55	1345.00	1,595.00
1200	Doors	853.00	112.54	113.00	740.00
1520	HVAC	240.00	350.00	350.00	(110.00)
1600	Electric	678.00	922.67	923.00	(245.00)
1700	Insulation	179.00	148.76	149.00	30.00
1800	Drywall	2127.00	2,096.26	2,097.00	32.00
2000	Millwork	436.00	1,201.53	1,201.00	(765.00)
2500	Clean Up	200.00	54.01	54.00	146.00
10000	Burden	0.00	864.42	864.00	(864.00)
		8,693.00	7,856.48	7,856.00	837.00

Solving Job Cost Overruns

Every remodeler battles cost overruns. They are inherent to this business and are the single most common reason remodelers are not profitable. Ninety percent of overruns will be in the labor category. That is logical since estimating labor is an act of judgment and the actual performance is subject to so many variables. If you can get your labor estimates and actuals to match up within 2%, you have done the hardest work. Here are some tips on solving job cost overruns:

Solve Labor Overruns...

- By discussing the estimated time or labor costs for each phase with the carpenter in charge of the project before work begins.

- By sharing the job cost reports with the Lead Carpenter so they can track, monitor and manage the labor, material and subs going into the project.

- By getting input on your estimates from the carpenter or production manager before your proposal is submitted.

- By requiring field personnel to keep daily time cards separating the job into phases so that overruns can be tracked and analyzed to the finest detail.

- By instituting an incentive program which splits any labor savings between the company and the lead carpenter.

Solve Subcontractor Overruns...

- By telling subs that they may visit every job before giving a price. If they choose not to do so, the risk of unknown (but foreseeable) conditions falls on them.

- By always getting fixed prices from your subs.

▨ By referencing your plans into your subcontractors' contracts.

▨ By asking that they let you know in writing (as part of their contract), if they are not including any labor or materials shown on the plans that would normally be in their area of specialty.

▨ By insisting subs let you know if there is a change that will cost extra to their contract before they actually perform the work. If they don't inform you beforehand, they don't get paid.

SOLVE MATERIAL OVERRUNS...

▨ By getting multiple prices on large material orders.

▨ By developing good supplier relationships.

▨ By asking for discounts on materials you buy frequently and in large quantities.

▨ By keeping careful estimating records for the purchaser to reference before they order.

▨ By avoiding wastage of valuable materials.
Have the person who estimated communicate to the lead carpenter just how the material usage (for instance, cuts) was figured.

▨ By using written confirmations with subs and suppliers that include specifications and pricing.

▨ By ordering ahead for supplier delivery and keeping in-house pickups to a bare minimum.

▨ By getting production personnel input during the estimating process.

Mine Strategic Information from Your Job Costs

If you only use your job costs to analyze each individual job, you are missing much of the potential qualitative information that can be gleaned from looking at the summary information on a year's worth of job costs.

By sorting your information you can learn:

■ Which categories you consistently underestimate.

■ Which type of jobs are most profitable.
Which are the least profitable.

■ Which dollar size job is most profitable.
Which is the least profitable.

■ Which lead carpenters' jobs come in best.
Which carpenters are unproductive.

■ Which salesperson sells the most profitable jobs.
Which sells the least profitable.

CUMULATIVE JOB COST REPORT

This report shows the final costs of 12 closed jobs and the gross profit these jobs produced. This type of report is very helpful because the data can be sorted to show gross profit on jobs of varying sizes or types, or jobs sold by different salespeople or even jobs constructed by different crews.

SAMPLE: CUMULATIVE JOB COST REPORT

JOB NAME	JOB TYPE	SOLD BY	AMOUNT OF CONTRACT	EST. SQS.	ACT. SQS.	+ / – SQS.	COST OF DIFF.
Carr	R	D	$ 4,500.00	24	24	0	$ 0.00
Reid	R	D	11,900.00	141	135	0	528.89
Black	W	D	2,750.00	11	11	0	0.00
Simms	Trim	M	1,491.00	1	1	0	0.00
Barry	W	M	1,435.00	2	2	0	0.00
Kreiser	R	D	3,625.00	28	27.7	.3	44.56
Pully	R	D	1,550.00	15	15	0	0.00
Garrett	W	D	2,400.00	1	1	0	0.00
Simpson	L	D	975.00	138	138	0	0.00
Oliver	L	D	840.00	143	151	-8	(44.50)
Downs	L	D	1,168.00	183	183	0	0.00
Hess	L	D	1,800.00	325	325	0	0.00

| **Summary** | | | **$ 34,434.00** | | | | |

COST OF MATERIAL	COST OF LABOR	LABOR PER UNIT	TAX ON LABOR	DUMP & MISC.	GROSS PROFIT	% GROSS PROFIT
$ 851.04	$ 1,555.00	$ 64.79	$ 93.30	$ 450.00	$ 1,643.96	37 %
4,462.49	1,469.00	10.88	88.14	—	5,968.51	50 %
1427.30	117.00	10.64	7.02	258.00	947.70	34 %
524.01	503.12	503.12	30.19	90.42	373.45	25 %
645.64	68.75	34.38	4.13	—	720.61	50 %
1,021.18	434.00	15.69	26.04	200.00	1,969.82	54 %
504.35	279.00	18.60	16.74	—	766.65	49 %
1,123.32	305.25	305.25	18.32	108.00	863.43	36 %
186.69	60.00	0.43	3.60	35.60	692.71	71 %
173.12	65.00	0.43	3.90	34.40	567.48	68 %
368.66	134.50	0.73	8.07	43.60	621.24	53 %
452.84	312.50	0.96	18.75	95.20	939.46	52 %
					$ 16,075.02	47 %

It takes considerable work to produce job costs manually but if you are not computerized, you must do it. Remember, once you are computerized, the production of job cost reports becomes a by-product of the other information you enter into your computer system. Computerization makes it simple to produce job costs daily if desired. But whether job costs are produced manually or through the power of the computer, they must be produced on a regular, timely basis for your company to flourish.

Some remodelers feel that if they do job cost reports, they can skip doing P & L statements. You need both. Track each job individually to assure that it produces the targeted gross profit (individual job cost report) and also make sure that all your jobs in concert produce the required gross profit (P & L). Your P & L also assures you that you are producing enough volume to pay your overhead. Go for both!

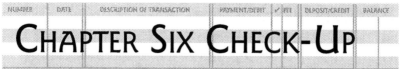

CHAPTER SIX CHECK-UP

1. What are the three reasons producing accurate job costs is so critical to a remodeler?

2. Once you see a job is running over budget, there's not much you can do to salvage that job.

☐ True   ☐ False

3. Your bookkeeper should not spend time breaking invoices into different job costs. That should be done by using one invoice per job.

☐ True   ☐ False

4. When your accounting is computerized, producing job costs becomes much easier.

☐ True   ☐ False

5. Ninety percent of job cost overruns will be found in the category of:

a. subcontractors

b. labor

c. materials

CHECK YOUR ANSWERS ON THE NEXT PAGE → → →

ANSWERS

1. The three reasons that producing accurate job costs is so critical are:

a. to help tighten cost control on the current job

b. to prevent overrruns on future jobs

c. to build a cost history for estimating

2. False. There are cost-cutting actions you can still take while the job is underway and you can be sure to charge for all changes to raise more revenue.

3. True. Save your bookkeeper's time by having the supplier (with the help of your personnel) use one invoice per job when writing up the order.

4. True. Assembling job costs becomes easier because the data needed has already been entered in the system for other accounting purposes.

5. Ninety percent of job cost overruns are found to be in the **labor** category.

Chapter 7

Forecasting Cash Flow

ood cash flow and profitability are two different entities and often do not coincide. Let me give you an example. Months of heavy construction volume mean you have the need for lots of cash to pay your labor and job costs. Often, draws do not keep up so while you may be earning profit you are not seeing it yet. These months may be followed by months of low construction volume when you are not earning as much profit but are collecting last payments and draws on new work. Your bank account is flush and you feel very optimistic. If you were to chart cash on hand and also chart your profits, you would find their cycles are quite different.

Cash Flow Pitfalls

One of the real advantages of being in remodeling instead of some other business is your ability to collect money before the job starts. A well run remodeling company has usually overbilled the buyer until the final bill. That final payment often represents the company's net profit. However, there are other occurrences that can rock the cash flow boat for a company. Here are just a few examples:

- Increasing volume very quickly.

- Experiencing a drop-off in new job contracts over a period of time.

- Taking a large job with draw schedules that are not favorable to the company.

- Taking jobs that have high retainage. For instance, architect supervised and commercial work often require that 10% of all draws be held until some specified time period after the job is finished.

- Leaving too much money to the end of the job to be collected and then having difficulty collecting that money.

- Investing too much money on non-liquid assets like equipment, trucks, or inventory in a warehouse.

- Moving to a new niche or diversification like Insurance Reconstruction where you often must finance the job until the end.

Running your company by reacting to the ebb and flow of cash is a very quick road to disaster. In *Every Manager's Guide to Business Finance*, Robert Finney advises "Cash flow remains important for any business of any size, because cash is the ultimate survival parameter. However, it is not the best financial measure of a business." An accurate P & L is your window on true profits. Yet, you must be aware of cash as well. Not having enough cash at the proper time has been a death knell to many a profitable company.

I remember consulting with a Midwest company early in my consulting career. It gave me such a vivid picture of the stranglehold poor cash flow takes on a company, that even 11 years later, I have not forgotten. The company was in a severe cash flow bind due to a string of unprofitable years. The remodeler was frantically selling jobs at or below cost in order to collect the initial draw and be able to deposit some money in his account. Hours each day were occupied with angry suppliers demanding money. These were non-productive hours and debilitating emotionally. The remodeler could buy from only certain suppliers and subs—not the best or least expensive, and not the suppliers or subs they wanted to buy from—because they had only a few accounts still open. It was a frightening situation and in spite of all we did, it was too late and the company did not survive.

Monitoring Cash Flow

It is difficult in remodeling to project cash flow accurately over a long period of time. I have watched a number of remodelers try but few have been successful. (The job you may be collecting money from in three months, you don't even know about today.) However, it can be very helpful to project cash flow for the next month or even one week at a time. This ability to forecast allows you to begin solving oncoming cash flow problems early. You may decide to speed up one job in order to collect a large draw. Or you may complete plans quickly so you can sign a new job. Or you may decide to hold off purchasing software or a truck for a month. Consider developing a Cash Flow Projector form (see sample) to predict your expected cash flow position over the next week (or month).

WEEKLY (MONTHLY) CASH FLOW PROJECTOR

Week (month) beginning _____

Beginning checkbook balance _____

INCOME:

SOURCE	AMOUNT	PICKUP DATE
_____	_____	_____
_____	_____	_____
_____	_____	_____
_____	_____	_____

Total Income $ _____

EXPENSES: (subs, suppliers, insurance, payroll and other)

PAYABLES WITH DISCOUNT

NAME	AMOUNT	DISCOUNT DATE
_____	_____	_____
_____	_____	_____
_____	_____	_____
_____	_____	_____

Subtotal $ _____

OTHER PAYABLES:

SOURCE	AMOUNT	DATE DUE
_____	_____	_____
_____	_____	_____
_____	_____	_____
_____	_____	_____

Total Income $ _____

Total expenses $ _____

Expected checkbook balance at end of week $ _____

(Beginning checkbook balance+ income – expenses)

If you are profitable over a period of time, you should be able to build up a cash reserve that reduces cash shortfalls and makes your business life less stressful. Yet even the most successful business usually has some periods during the year when cash must be hoarded and carefully doled out.

Tips for Maximizing Cash Flow

THE GOLDEN RULES OF CASH FLOW

There are three golden rules of cash flow that all businesses must obey. They are:
- collect early
- pay as late as you can without damaging credit
- be profitable

Following the three golden rules of cash flow, here are 15 tried and true tips for creating favorable cash flow in your business—assuming you are also profitable! They fall under 4 categories:

1. optimizing contract draws
2. collecting smartly
3. buying carefully
4. excelling as a money manager

Optimize Contract Draws

1. If you are using draws based on job progress, always word those draws to become due **upon start of a phase** rather than **completion of,** and you will maximize your cash and minimize your arguments with the customer. In doing this, you do not have to change the timing of the draw. For instance, you can substitute "upon start of trim" for "upon completion of drywall." You are simply trying to make the draws less open to interpretation.

2. Collect a first draw that is fair to the buyer but gives you as much leverage as possible. Review state law. Often remodelers ask for 20-30% down with mid-size jobs, 50% with small jobs. If the job is particularly material-heavy, consider a larger first draw. Remodelers will typically collect 50% of the contract before commencement in kitchen remodelings to compensate for the large volume of special materials that must be ordered.

3. Split the final draw into two smaller draws—the first is substantial completion (when the space is ready for occupancy) and a smaller draw upon completion of the punchlist. Don't let other charges like change orders, selections and time and material charges fall into the final draws. Be sure to bill them as early as possible.

4. Some remodelers collect draws based on a time period. They may collect every week or every two weeks. If the Basehart job is a $12,000 job and is expected to take six weeks, the remodeler will collect $2000 a week. If there is a delay, the draw schedule will be adjusted. This type of draw is very helpful for foreseeing incoming cash flow.

5. An increasing number of remodelers who work on a cost plus or time and materials basis are requesting a substantial "retainer" before they begin the job and are working draws against that retainer which is very helpful for cash flow.

Be a Smart Collector

6. Hand deliver invoices and personally pick up checks. Over a year's period, this practice will make major inroads on cash flow problems.

7. Make bill collecting a person-to-person effort. Do not just make and send additional invoices. Phone, discuss, and meet the customer in person to settle any confusion, questions or problems quickly.

8. When doing work for another business such as commercial work or insurance reconstruction, find out at contract signing who will approve bills and pay them—and ask about the firm's payment procedures. Different offices may have to approve an invoice before it is paid. An invoice may need two or three signatures. Knowing the system allows the remodeler to expedite payment. Faxing two invoices may help: one for the person supervising construction and one for the person actually approving payments. Find out the client's preferred system and work within it to obtain prompt payment.

Be a Foxy Buyer

9. Always pay discounted bills in time to take the discount. That percentage you save for spending your money 20 days earlier is a bargain. Do it. Pay other bills on the last date that will maintain the firm's good credit.

10. Subcontract rather than employ when possible. Sub-contractors are often paid only one or two times during a job whereas your own labor may be paid each week.

11. Rather than purchasing in cash or on account, consider using credit cards that give you a rebate or airline mileage where possible. When charges are paid off monthly on some credit cards, the purchases are interest-free and they extend credit to the company for a month or more. However, don't let this get out of hand and get you into debt. These fifteen tips are meant to smooth cash flow — not tempt you into deep indebtedness.

12. If you do not have supplier accounts now, see if you are eligible for them. A monthly account may save you money both through the extended credit and through the available discounts.

Excel as a Money Manager

13. Consider bi-weekly payroll. You'll increase your cash float while cutting the cost of doing payroll in half. Thousands of remodelers have accomplished this successfully and, yes, field personnel can make the adjustment.

14. As your volume gets larger, you may want to develop a line of credit with a bank that can be used to smooth out the firm's cash needs. Think of a line of credit only as a short term bridge loan—not to get you out of financial trouble—but to allow you to take work that requires your temporary financing of the job. Clean up—by paying up—your line of credit once a year.

15. Watch warehousing. Does the savings from buying in quantity and stocking frequently used material really surpass the cost of space, of inventorying, and of tracking damage to stored materials? Inventory ties up cash.

Cash flow can be your friend or foe. I've seen remodeling businesses devastated by lack of cash. The owner's focus becomes robbing Peter to pay Paul instead of running an effective business. However, if you are running your company with a loss currently, let me cheer you by telling you that I've seen remodelers make striking comebacks with the help of excellent money management.

Build up some capital in your firm. That will reduce stress on you more than almost any other act you can take. Remember, cash flow is your friend.

CHAPTER SEVEN CHECK-UP

1. Companies have cash flow problems because they aren't profitable.

☐ True   ☐ False

2. List the three golden rules of cash flow.

3. By writing contract draws carefully, you can improve your cash flow.

☐ True   ☐ False

4. What are two ideas you could use in purchasing to improve your cash flow?

5. Remodelers have been unsuccessful in paying personnel every two weeks because employees are unwilling to wait for their pay.

☐ True   ☐ False

CHECK YOUR ANSWERS ON THE NEXT PAGE → → →

ANSWERS

1. False. Even profitable companies can have cash flow crises.

2. The three golden rules of cash flow are a) collect early, b) pay late but keep your credit excellent, c) be profitable.

3. True. There are many ways you can improve cash flow by carefully wording contract draws.

4 You could improve your cash flow by checking pricing carefully, paying discounted bills in time to get the discount, by subcontracting wherever possible, by using accounts or credit cards instead of cash and by avoiding warehousing.

5. False. Many remodelers pay all their personnel every other week and have cut their payroll preparation costs in half and had better cash flow as a result.

Chapter 8

Budgeting: Your Plan for Profit

"My wife wanted a new fur coat and I wanted a new car. We couldn't afford both of them so we compromised. We bought the fur coat, but we keep it in the garage."

Anonymous

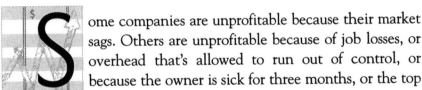ome companies are unprofitable because their market sags. Others are unprofitable because of job losses, or overhead that's allowed to run out of control, or because the owner is sick for three months, or the top salesperson leaves taking some jobs with him. But there's one situation that is the saddest of all.

Sometimes after reviewing the remodeler's financial reports and analyzing their complete operation, I can look at them and tell them that nothing they "did" all year made them unprofitable. That, instead, they are losing money because of the "formula" they were working under. Had they tried out this formula on paper on January 1, they would have seen that it wouldn't work for them. What a waste!

Making money calls for working smart, not working hard. You must build in to each job and in to your company operation, the money it takes to run your operation profitably. And you do that by creating a formula or recipe that—at least on paper—will leave you with profit at the end of the year.

If you can't make your operation work on paper, it won't work in real life. If you can make it work on paper, you have a good chance of making it work in the real world.

Remodelers are doers. They're action-oriented. They'll make it happen by pushing and pulling. Paper planning doesn't come naturally. But doing some paperwork here will save you a year of grief. That seems like an excellent exchange.

Budgets Prevent Problems

For three years Jim Meehan had been frustrated. Each year he wanted his remodeling business to complete $1.2 million in volume. In January of each year, it looked like this would be the year his business would achieve that desired volume. Jim would staff up, design the marketing program, and coach his team to work hard each week and month. But by the end of the third quarter he would begin to see the inevitable signs that his company would hit just under $1 million in volume.

Because his overhead was sized to a $1.2 million volume each year, a volume shortfall to $1 million meant no profits. It meant another breakeven year where Jim made his salary but that was all. So in 1995, Jim decided planning would be the key to ending the no-profit years. He learned about budgeting and how creating a "what if" budget could allow him to see early on what volume was needed to sustain a certain amount of overhead and yet still yield the net profit he wanted. Planning would help him rework his overhead quickly to fit any unforeseen occurence.

If Jim found that he was not going to reach his desired volume, he could cut overhead early in the year. He was using a plan on paper—his budget—to test his idea and then to be his roadmap to profitability. It worked.

SAMPLE "WHAT-IF" BUDGET

A "What-if" Budget allows you to check the outcome of different volumes—in this case four, ranging from $1 million to $1.2 million. Sometimes, this type of budget shows you that you are more profitable at a lower volume—particularly if the higher volume requires that you hire more office or managerial personnel.

This budget confirmed what Jim knew, that to reach the highest profit, he needed to produce the $1.25 volume. Even then, his net profit would not be the suggested 10%, but 7%.

John Doe Design Remodeling Inc.
Operating Budget 1995, what ifs

INCOME

Direct Contracts	1,235,000	98.80%	1,185,000	98.75%	1,088,000	98.91%	1,010,000	99.02%
Design Contracts	15,000	1.20	15,000	1.25	12,000	1.09	10,000	0.98
TOTAL INCOME	**1,250,000**	**100.00**	**1,200,000**	**100.00**	**1,100,000**	**100.00**	**1,020,000**	**100.00**

JOB COSTS

Direct labor	174,503	13.97	167,600	13.97	153,633	13.97	142,460	13.97
Direct labor payroll taxes	16,875	1.35	16,200	1.35	14,850	1.35	13,770	1.35
Workman's comp.ins. (dir. labor)	25,000	2.00	24,000	2.00	22,000	2.00	20,400	2.00
Employee uniforms	4,583	0.37	4,400	0.37	4,033	0.37	3,740	0.37
Subcontractors	197,917	15.83	190,000	15.83	174,167	15.83	161,500	15.83
Materials	312,500	25.00	300,000	25.00	275,000	25.00	255,000	25.00
Equipment Rent	625	0.05	600	0.05	550	0.05	510	0.05
Landfill fees	10,417	0.83	10,000	0.83	9,167	0.83	8,500	0.83
Drawing–Plans	10,417	0.83	10,000	0.83	9,167	0.83	8,500	0.83
Building permits	1,583	0.13	1,520	0.13	1,393	0.13	1,292	0.13
TOTAL JOB COSTS	**754,500**	**60.36%**	**724,320**	**60.36**	**663,960**	**60.36**	**615,672**	**60.36**
GROSS PROFIT	**495,500**	**39.64%**	**475,680**	**39.64**	**436,040**	**39.64**	**404,328**	**39.64**

John Doe Design Remodeling Inc.
Operating Budget 1995, what ifs

OPERATING EXPENSES

Officer/office salaries	70,000	5.60%	70,000	5.83%	70,000	6.36%	70,000	6.86%
Sales salaries	87,500	7.00	84,000	7.00	77,000	7.00	71,400	7.00
Designer salaries	11,440	0.92	11,440	0.95	11,440	1.04	11,440	1.12
Maintenance labor	3,125	0.25	3,000	0.25	2,750	0.25	2,550	0.25
Production salaries (part year)	20,195	1.61	20,195	1.68	20,195	1.83	20,195	1.97
Admin. labor	3,792	0.30	3,640	0.30	3,337	0.30	3,094	0.30
Payroll tax expense	16,483	1.32	15,824	1.32	14,505	1.32	13,450	1.32
Tax penalties	0	0.00	0	0.00	0	0.00	0	0.00
Employee health insurance	6,250	0.50	6,000	0.50	5,500	0.50	5,100	0.50
Health insurance	4,800	0.38	4,800	0.40	4,800	0.44	4,800	0.47
Life insurance	750	0.06	750	0.06	750	0.07	750	0.07
Employee education expense	3,125	0.25	3,000	0.25	2,750	0.25	2,550	0.25
Training expense	2,083	0.17	2,000	0.17	1,833	0.17	1,700	0.17
Business entertainment	3,125	0.25	3,000	0.25	2,750	0.25	2,550	0.25
Marketing/advertising	52,083	4.17	50,000	4.17	45,833	4.17	42,500	4.17
Marketing labor	2,917	0.23	2,800	0.23	2,567	0.23	2,380	0.23
Bad debts	3,125	0.25	3,000	0.25	2,750	0.25	2,550	0.25
Depreciation expense	16,667	1.32	16,000	1.33	14,667	1.32	13,600	1.32
Dues & subscriptions	2,083	0.17	2,000	0.17	1,833	0.17	1,700	0.1P
Disability insurance	1,721	0.14	1,721	0.14	1,721	0.16	1,721	0.17
Liability insurance	3,798	0.30	3,646	0.30	3,342	0.30	3,099	0.30
Workmans comp insurance (office)	2,604	0.21	2,500	0.21	2,292	0.21	2,125	0.21
Vehicle insurance	5,208	0.42	5,000	0.42	4,583	0.42	4,250	0.42
Legal & accounting	4,688	0.38	4,500	0.38	4,125	0.38	3,825	0.38
Shop expense	938	0.08	900	0.08	825	0.08	765	0.08
Office expense	13,437	1.07	12,900	1.08	11,825	1.07	10,965	1.08
Postage expense	2,958	0.24	2,840	0.24	2,603	0.24	2,414	0.24
Rent expense	16,000	1.28	16,000	1.33	16,000	1.45	16,000	1.57
Supplies expense	2,083	0.17	2000	0.17	1,833	0.17	1,700	0.17
Tool repair	500	0.04	480	0.04	440	0.04	408	0.04
Sales promotion	0	0.00	0	0.00	0	0.00	0	0.00
Telephone	8,208	0.66	7,880	0.66	7,224	0.66	6,699	0.66
Travel expense	4,168	0.33	4,000	0.33	3,667	0.33	3,400	0.33

John Doe Design Remodeling Inc.
Operating Budget 1995, what ifs

Utilities	500	0.04%	500	0.04%	500	0.05%	500	0.05%
Vehicle expense	25,000	2.00	24,000	2.00	22,000	2.00	20,400	2.00
Warranty costs	6,250	0.50	6,000	0.50	5,500	0.50	5,100	0.50
Total Operating Expenses	**407,604**	**32.61%**	**396,316**	**33.03%**	**373,740**	**33.98%**	**355,680**	**34.87%**
NET INCOME	**87,896**	**7.03%**	**79,364**	**6.61%**	**62,300**	**5.66**	**48,648**	**4.77%**
BREAK EVEN								
Overhead	407,604		396,316		373,740		355,680	
Divided by GP	39.64%		39.64%		39.64%		39.64%	
Break even/yr	1,028,264		999,788		942,836		897,275	
Break even/mth	85,689		83,316		78,570		74,773	

Planning for Profit

The dictionary defines budget as an itemized summary of probable expenditures and income for a given period, usually including a systematic plan for meeting expenses. Another way to think of a budget is a **plan for profit.** Profit is so elusive, so easy to wear away or lose all together, that it takes superhuman effort in a company **to protect the bottom line.** A budget is your best line of defense in planning for and protecting your profit.

David Bangs, Jr., in *Financial Troubleshooting*, emphasizes just how critical budgets are to a business: "Businesses which use tight, carefully thought out budgets succeed. If they stumble, they can be picked up, dusted off, and sent forward—but businesses without budgets collapse without a chance to redeem themselves."

Most remodelers avoid creating a budget because

- "Remodeling is so variable I can't control what I sell."

- "I don't know my numbers well enough to project ahead."

- "The idea of budgeting makes me squirm. I would have to watch and account for every penny. No thanks!"

Robert Finney, author of *Every Manager's Guide to Business Finance*, answers "There is no way to take uncertainty out of the future. The right way to deal with it is to recognize it, plan the work intelligently, make assumptions for the important factors that are uncertain and uncontrollable, and use the best available sources for budget numbers."

It's time to put your excuses away. If you're tired of saying "why is there so much month left at the end of the money?", if you want to be able to track and monitor your road to profitability, you'll embrace the balanced budget. You are going to be amazed just how easy it is to create your own plan for profit.

Six Steps to Creating a Balanced Budget

1. **Start with volume.** As you can see from the sample budget, base all budgets on a particular volume. Without that anchoring point, you have no idea what resources, people, office space, or supplies will be needed to produce those dollars. If you are unsure of the volume that is realistic to plan, do as the sample shows and create three or four "what-ifs."

   Volume is partially in your hands (How much do you want to do? How much can you do well? What are you willing to walk away from?) and is partially in the hands of your marketplace. Consider both these factors in your planning. If you're not sure, consider doing what Jim did and look at a variety of volume levels.

2. **Next figure job costs as a percentage of that volume.** Look at job costs from two angles.

   First, what will your markup be? That will create a targeted job cost percentage (as the chart in chapter 3 shows, a markup of 50% targets a 67% job cost, a markup of 60% targets job costs of 62.5%).

   Secondly, find out whether you have been coming in on these targets in the past. Let's say that your 50% markup has been in effect for 3 years. While you have been targeting job costs of 67%, you have actually been getting job costs of 75% overall. Therefore, consider not just targeted performance but actual performance.

   In the above scenario, you might want to budget for 75% job costs or—even better—budget for 72% and create a strong action plan for how you and your team will bring those job costs into close alignment with your intended percentages. That plan might include improving field performance, analyzing estimating accuracy, better subcontractor and material purchasing control. Most importantly, be conservative in taking savings before you have achieved them!

3. **Next figure your overhead.** Here, don't use percentages. Instead, line item each expenditure based on your expenses from last year. You can often use the overhead list from your Profit and Loss statement (see chapter 3). If you have a "what-if" budget, you'll find that overhead changes only minimally with volume except when you are forced to add personnel.

4. **Next figure extraordinary expenditures.** Maybe you want to purchase a new computer or software, or a dump truck. What do you intend to do this coming year to get the money to invest in these items that you didn't do this current year? Include your wish list for a new desk or new office space. You may have to cut this when you get to step 6 but include it for now.

5. **Figure 8-10 % for the net profit line.** Often in budgeting, you get to this line and can squeeze out only 2 or 3%. Don't settle for this. Because actual job costs are often higher than budgeted costs, a 2-3% net profit line will usually erode into a breakeven year or even a loser. You must figure an 8-10% net profit and this is after your salary is included in either job costs or overhead.

6. **Call this the "whoops" step.** Often your budget numbers add up to more than 100%. The bank (and the budget) are broke. You have to go around again and balance your budget. It is extremely rare to develop a balanced budget on the first try.

(Now stop for a moment. If you had just worked your way blindly through the year with no planning, you would have been in a mess. You've been smart to work this out on paper first. Congratulate yourself!)

To make your budget work, review overhead (can you do with less?) and especially your extraordinary expenditures (can we put these unusual investments off for a year - or indefinitely?). What can be cut? If your budget is still out of balance see what you can do by:

- raising markup a few percentage points

- raising volume a bit

- reducing job costs a few percentage points with a workable action plan

Often the best solution involves using all of the above adjustments.

FIGURING BREAKEVEN

Breakeven is the point at which all your gross profit goes for overhead and there is no net profit. It is not a happy occurrence, but it beats losing money. Figure what your breakeven volume is for the year or the month by dividing your overhead dollars for that period by your gross profit percentage.

Example: You want to know what your breakeven volume for the year is. Your overhead will run you $100,000 while your gross profit is expected to run 35%:

$$\frac{\$100,000}{.35} = \$285,714$$

You must produce $285,714 in volume at a 35% gross profit in order to breakeven—pay all your job cost bills and all your overhead bills. There will be no money left for net profit.

Budgets and Teampower

Your budget can be an important unifying document for your staff. They should help plan it and then implement it. While a budget is full of numbers, those numbers represent goals, dreams, wants and needs.

Get the maximum benefit from your budget by:

1. Holding monthly or quarterly reviews in which everyone in your company participates.

2. Tying incentives to budget goals. Everyone should have some financial stake in making the plan happen.

3. Educating all personnel on the financial realities of your business. Only then can they contribute fully to helping you make the profit that creates the job security and opportunity that they desire.

Quarterly Budget Review

Once you have developed this roadmap to profit, you're ready to get to work to make it actually happen. If you can, build an "estimated" or "budgeted" column into your monthly Profit and Loss statement (see sample). Compare your budget vs. actual performance at least quarterly. Always insist that the budget be accurate with what we know today and that it be adjusted whenever we learn some new financial fact that will change a budget category. Each November begin the budgeting process for the new year.

BUDGET TO ACTUAL COMPARISON INCOME STATEMENT

This report—from an actual remodeler—contrasts a six month P & L total with the budget totals projected for that six month period. The Net Income actually ran $10,000 higher than budgeted.

BUDGET TO ACTUAL COMPARISON
INCOME STATEMENT
— 6 months

	Current Balance	Current Percent	Budget Balance	Budget Percent	Dollar Variance	Percent Variance
Commercial Operations Income	$ 38,079.80	7.32 %	$ 9,999.96	2.00 %	$ (28,079.84)	$ (280.80)
Residential Operations Income	475,494.25	91.35	484,999.98	96.84	9,505.73	1.96
Anderson Window Repair	0.00-	0.00	0.00	0	0.00	0
Design Services Income	6,328.03	1.22	4,999.98	1.00	(1,328.05)	(26.56)
Comp. Annual Premium Discount	0.00	0.00	0.00	0	0.00	0
Trade Discounts	586.73	.11	799.98	.16	213.25	26.66
TOTAL INCOME	**$ 520,488.81**	**100.00%**	**$500,799.90**	**100%**	**(19,688.91)**	**$ (3.93)**
DIRECT COSTS						
Direct Materials	$ 75,606.13	14.53%	90,000.00	17.97%	$ 14,393.87	$ 15.99
Subcontractor Costs	207,685.61	39.90	167,499.96	33.45	(40,185.65)	(23.99)
Direct Labor	32,762.74	6.29	33,003.96	6.59	241.22	.73
Tool Rental Allowance	49.50	.01	500.00	.10	450.50	90.10
Direct Labor Vehicle Allowance	960.00	.19	960.00	.19	0.00	0.00
Prod. Vac/Holiday Pay	1,356.00	.26	1,596.00	.32	240.00	15.04
Prod. FICA-ER	2,694.49	.51	2,725.98	.54	31.49	1.16
Prod. FUTA	165.54	.04	264.00	.06	98.46	37.30
Prod. SUTA	448.87	.08	280.98	.05	(167.89)	(59.75)
Prod. Workers Comp.	4,394.82	.85	5,604.00	1.12	1,209.18	21.58
Production Vehicle Fuel	1,053.64	.20	980.00	.20	(73.64)	(7.51)
Prod. Vehicle Maint/Repair	636.72	.12	679.96	.13	43.24	6.36
Equipment Rentals	637.33	.12	999.96	.20	362.63	36.26
Site Utilities	0.00	0.00	49.98	.01	49.98	100.00
Site Sanitation/Landfill	2,969.88	.58	3,000.00	.60	30.12	1.00
Building Permits	1,644.51	.31	1,500.00	.30	(144.51)	(9.63)
Plans/Design Costs	4,180.26	.80	3,750.00	.75	(430.26)	(11.47)
Gen. Liab. Ins.-Carpenters	2,507.92	.49	1,549.50	.31	(958.42)	(61.85)
Gen. Liab. Ins.-Tools & Equip.	94.01	.01	94.01	.02	0.00	0.00

BUDGET TO ACTUAL COMPARISON
INCOME STATEMENT
— 6 months

	Current Balance	Current Percent	Budget Balance	Budget Percent	Dollar Variance	Percent Variance
Gen. Liab. Ins.-Subcontractors	1,212.49	.24	1,212.49	.24	0.00	0
Production Supplies/Materials	838.22	.16	720.00	.14	(118.22)	(16.42)
Prod. Equipment Maint/Repair	0.00-	0.00	99.96	.02	99.96	100.00
Other Direct Expenses	122.14	.02	120.00	.03	(2.14)	(1.78)
TOTAL JOB COSTS	**$ 342,020.82**	**65.71%**	**$317,190.74**	**63.34%**	**($24,830.08)**	**(7.83)%**
GROSS MARGIN	**$ 178,467.99**	**34.29%**	**$183,609.16**	**36.66%**	**$5,141.17**	**2.80 %**

EXPENSES

	Current Balance	Current Percent	Budget Balance	Budget Percent	Dollar Variance	Percent Variance
Officer Salary	$ 31,000.00	5.96%	$ 31,000.00	6.19%	0	0
Office Salaries/Wages	18,969.25	3.64	18,661.98	3.72	(307.27)	(1.65)
Office Vacation/Holiday	1,092.75	.21	1,087.98	.22	(4.77)	(.44)
Office Bonuses	50.00	.01	0.00	0	(50.00)	0.00
Prod. Manager Salary	21,600.00	4.15	21,274.98	4.25	(325.02)	(1.53)
Prod. Mgr Vac/Holiday Pay	1,800.00	.35	2,124.96	.42	324.96	15.29
Sales/Commissions/Finder Fees	17,080.50	3.28	30,000.00	5.99	12,919.50	43.07
Employee Perks/Bonuses	303.30	.06	240.00	.05	(63.30)	(26.38)
Subcontractor Perks/Bonuses	30.00	0.00	300.00	.06	270.00	90.00
FICA-ER	6,948.35	1.34	5,346.00	1.07	(1,602.35)	(29.97)
FUTA	202.62	.04	214.00	.04	11.38	5.32
SUTA	801.86	.15	812.00	.16	10.14	1.25
Workers Comp.	966.66	.19	1,338.96	.27	372.30	27.81
Direct Building Expense	12.10	0.00	48.00	.01	35.90	74.79
Architect/Design	20.00	0.00	168.00	.03	148.00	88.10
Photography	270.33	.05	240.00	.05	(30.33)	(12.64)
Office Veh. Fuel	450.73	.09	412.50	.08	(38.23)	(9.27)
Office Veh. Insurance	227.79	.04	210.00	.05	(17.39)	(8.28)
Office Veh. Maint/Repair	175.23	.04	75.00	.01	(100.23)	(133.64)
Office Veh. Depr.	2,042.16	.39	2,042.10	.41	(.06)	0.00
Office Equip. Depr.	1,328.72	.26	1,187.52	.24	(141.20)	11.89
General Liability	240.00	.04	240.00	.04	0.00	0.00
Accounting	1,150.00	.22	900.00	.18	(250.00)	(27.78)
Advertising	- 0 -	0.00	60.00	.02	60.00	100.00
Bank Charges	24.00	.01	96.00	.02	72.00	75.00
Charitable Contributions	66.50	.01	180.00	.03	113.50	63.06
Communications	4,387.67	.84	3,399.96	.68	(987.71)	(29.05)
Computer Expenses	3,353.34	.65	3,105.00	.62	(248.34)	(8.00)
Dues & Subscriptions	$ 389.95	.07%	54.54	.01	(335.41)	(614.98)
Education	1,973.37	.38	2,439.96	.49	466.59	19.12

BUDGET TO ACTUAL COMPARISON
INCOME STATEMENT
— 6 months

	Current Balance	Current Percent	Budget Balance	Budget Percent	Dollar Variance	Percent Variance
Group Health Insurance	1,213.28	.24	1,248.00	.25	34.72	2.78
Medical Insurance Supplement	900.00	.17	900.00	.18	0.00	0.00
Group Disability Insurance .	700.45	.13	670.00	.13	(30.45)	(4.54)
Legal	(770.34)	(.15)	600.00	.12	1,370.34	228.39
Marketing	2,843.84	.55	4,999.98	1.00	2,156.14	43.12
Meals & Entertainment	629.75	.12	600.00	.12	(29.75)	(4.96)
Office Rent	3,600.00	.69	3,600.00	.72	0.00	0.00
Office Maint/Repair	262.31	.05	360.00	.07	97.69	27.14
Office Supplies	1,214.75	.24	780.00	.16	(434.75)	(55.74)
Office Equipment Maint/Repair	155.35	.03	390.00	.07	234.65	60.17
Postage	842.59	.16	390.00	.08	(452.59)	(116.05)
Shop Rent	2,484.00	.48	2,484.00	.50	0.00	0.00
Shop Maint/Repair	164.55	.03	300.00	.06	135.45	45.15
Small Tools	426.02	.08	499.98	.10	73.96	14.79
Tool Maint/Repair	163.95	.03	249.96	.05	86.01	34.41
Travel	1,852.97	.36	1,999.98	.40	147.01	7.35
Trade Associations	75.00	.01	75.00	.01	0.00	0.00
Utilities	1,195.64	.23	1,200.00	.24	4.36	.36
Other Operating Expenses	0.00	0.00	120.00	.02	120.00	100.00
Uniforms	577.50	.11	199.98	.04	(377.52)	(188.00)
Other Expenses.	0.00	0.00	300.00	.06	300.00	100.00
TOTAL EXPENSES	**$ 135,488.39**	**26.03%**	**$149,226.32**	**29.80%**	**$13,737.93**	**9.21**
NET INCOME BEFORE OTHER INCOME	**$ 42,979.60**	**8.26%**	**$ 34,382.84**	**6.87%**	**$ (8,596.76)**	**(25.00)**
Interest Income	898.17	.17%	$ 360.00	.07	$ (538.17)	(149.49)
Brokerage Interest Income	1,797.00	.35	2,040.00	.40	243.00	11.91
Dividend Income	5,393.00	1.03	5,393.00	1.08	0.00	0.00
Other Income	1,908.19	.37	600.00	.12	(1,308.19)	(218.03)
Total Other Income	$ 9,996.36	1.92%	$ 8,393.00	1.68	$ (1,603.36)	(19.10)
NET INCOME (LOSS) BEFORE TAXES	**$ 52,975.96**	**10.18%**	**$42,775.84**	**8.54**	**$ (10,200.12)**	**(23.85)**
Income Taxes	2,920.00	.56	2,080.00	.41	(840.00)	(40.38)
NET INCOME (LOSS)	**$ 50,055.96**	**9.62%**	**$ 40,695.84**	**8.13%**	**$ (9,360.12)**	**(23.00)**

A budget is like your estimate for Mrs. Witter's porch enclosure—only it estimates what it will cost to run your company for a year. Your Profit & Loss statement is like your actual job cost for your company. We know you can do that porch enclosure estimate—and so we know you can do a great "planning for profit" budget!

Now's the time to follow the budget and make it happen. Don't be like George Allen, the former coach of the Washington Redskins football team. Team owner Edward Bennett Williams said of Allen "I gave him an unlimited budget and he exceeded it."

CHAPTER EIGHT CHECK-UP

1. Another way to look at a budget is as a plan for _____.

2. If you aren't sure what your volume will be for the coming year, just omit that information from your budget.

☐ True   ☐ False

3. In figuring your job costs, use the percentage of costs targeted by your markup even if your job costs consistently run over the estimated percentage.

☐ True   ☐ False

4. Always figure a net profit of _____% to _____%.

5. You often have to refigure a budget more than once to get it to balance.

☐ True   ☐ False

6. Your overhead is running $25,000 a month and you generate a 30% gross profit. What is your breakeven volume each month?

7. Only large volume remodelers will benefit from budgeting.

☐ True   ☐ False

CHECK YOUR ANSWERS ON THE NEXT PAGE ➔ ➔ ➔

ANSWERS

1. Another way to look at a budget is as a *plan for profit*.

2. False. Volume sets the stage for every other number in the budget. You cannot omit it.

3. False. In figuring your likely job cost percentage, use a number between the percentage of costs targeted by your markup and the actual job cost percentage that you achieve.

4. Always figure a net profit of 8-10%.

5. True. You often have to refigure a budget more than once to get it to balance.

6. Divide your overhead dollars by the gross profit percentage to get breakeven.

$$\frac{\$25,000}{.30} = \$83,333.$$

Thus you need $83,333 in volume each month just to break even.

7. False. Every business, of whatever size, will benefit from budgeting to show how they intend to make a profit.

Chapter 9

Your Financial Team

"I am often asked who the most important person in my business is. I would like to think it is me, one of the carpenters, or my foreman. However, I have to admit that the most important person is the bookkeeper. I can sell the jobs, hire the people to do the jobs, and buy the material. But, if I do not know what my overhead is, everything I have done is in vain."

Jud Motsenbocker,
<u>Managing the Small Construction Business</u>

While, as owner, you always remain the financial manager of your company, you depend on a team of at least two to assemble the data and make sure it is accurate. This team presents that data to you in an industry approved format that makes it an easy-to-use management tool. That team is your bookkeeper and your accountant.

The Bookkeeper

Usually—but not always—the bookkeeper is an in-house employee who handles the assembling of data and its entry into the system. Your bookkeeper should be experienced and able to prepare the monthly profit and loss statements and balance sheets as well as the job cost reports. Your bookkeeper should be your "right arm" who is thinking for—and ahead—of you when it comes to financial matters in the company. If you have to think ahead of your bookkeeper, you have the wrong bookkeeper.

From years of working with hundreds of companies, I have found that the job of bookkeeper is likely to be half time in a million dollar specialty company and close to full time in a million dollar full line remodeling company. Computerizing enhances the accuracy, speed and variety of reports you receive but does not usually reduce the bookkeeper's time. Usually, you as owner want more and more financial information generated as you begin to see the power and usefulness of reports in managing your company.

One option that may help your company if your volume is small, is to subcontract your bookkeeping. Some accountants have bookkeepers on staff who will work parttime for clients. Or there are freelance bookkeepers who will come in to your office and work a few hours each week. Some take your books back to their office and keep your data on their computer.

Another option that may help you minimize the in-office time spent on your bookkeeping is to use a payroll service to generate paychecks and the government reports based on payroll. Since producing payroll is very labor intensive for your office, this is often a time and money saver and reduces the bookkeeping load. Many payroll services can give you payroll data on disc to enter into your computerized job costing and accounting programs.

EMBEZZLEMENT ALERT!

You'd be surprised how many remodelers have had money stolen from them by an employee who had access to their checks and bookkeeping system. To avoid the pain and agony of an embezzlement, take these simple precautions:

1. Have bank statements sent to your home. Open them and review the checks for any discrepancy.

2. Sign checks personally and ask that all backup information be attached to the check for you to review if you desire.

3. Sign-off on on the backup information so that the same item can't be presented to you twice.

4. Review bank deposits to make sure all checks are being deposited.

5. Every now and then, look in the bookkeeping files to make sure old bills and checks are not being squirreled away.

6. Review the outstanding check list on the bank reconciliation to make sure the bookkeeper is not holding checks back.

7. Review and challenge job cost reports regularly.

8. Protect your checks. Many instances of stealing involve taking checks from the back of the checkbook where their absence won't be noticed. Don't ride around with a checkbook unprotected in your truck.

Check with your bank for their additional recommendations.

Your bookkeeper stays in close contact with your accountant who is a more highly trained (and paid) professional. Between them they should work amicably to provide the information you need to manage your company. If you don't understand something on your reports, ask! You are paying considerable money to assemble the data. Be sure to use it as your most strategic weapon in transforming your company.

The Accountant

Why should you have an outside accountant? A jokester once said that an accountant is a person hired to explain that you didn't make the money you thought you did. In reality, you hire an accountant to give you an independent opinion on your financial data. You also want that data formatted to meet accepted and universal accounting principles. You want various reports prepared accurately for tax purposes and good advice on managing your company based on that data.

Hopefully you have a friend and valued advisor in your accountant. If not, change accountants. Look for an accountant who already has clients in your industry. That way, other remodeling businesses will have paid to educate the accountant on your industry and you will reap the benefits. Consider asking your local association or remodelers you respect for recommendations.

Look for a roll-up-your-sleeves type of person who enjoys servicing small businesses and understands their special needs. Remember that your accountant is your most conservative advisor. Always consider their advice from that viewpoint.

Who's in Charge?

Robert Townsend, the former president of Avis-Rent-a-Car advises "Accountants can be smarter than anybody else or more ambitious or both, but essentially they are bean counters — their job is to serve the operation. They can't run the ship." Who's in charge? Without doubt, you are.

You need financial documentation that gives you the information you want when you want it. Once computerized, your financial data can be presented in any number of report types. Work with your accountant to choose the format you want— there are lots of alternatives. Many times remodelers don't use their financial reports because they aren't presented in a format that lends itself to easy analysis in this business. The reports used as illustrations throughout this book are excellent examples of what you might want to request from your accountant.

Accounting Services

Talk to your accountant about the level of service that best fits your needs, company size and budget. There are three levels of service:

- Audits
- Reviews
- Compilations

ACCOUNTING SERVICE MENU

TYPE	COST	SERVICE
Audits	Expensive	Accountant verifies much of your data independently and expresses an opinion in the reports of its accuracy.
Reviews	Moderate	Accountant reviews your data to a limited degree and expresses a limited opinion as to its accuracy. Often this is the minimum level required by lenders.
Compilations	Frugal	Accountant presents your data in an accepted format without an attempt to verify its accuracy. Used by most remodeling companies.

Most remodelers request compilations from their accountants unless some outside business need exists for a higher level of service. However, Steve Maltzman, CPA, of Construction Accounting Services in Colton, CA., says "I don't recommend that remodelers get audits or reviews unless required by an outside party. A compilation really isn't even necessary if the remodeler is using their accountant as a regular advisor throughout the year."

Hold Regular Meetings

If I have one message, it is this: Take control of your own financial future. Be sure to meet with your bookkeeper at least weekly to review company finances and reports. Meet with the accountant quarterly or semi-annually to review your company performance and get advice on tax issues and company financial status. You don't need to know how to assemble the numbers—others are much better at that than you. You must know how to analyze the numbers—no one is better or cares more about your business than you do.

Your bookkeeper and accountant are your financial team. Be sure they are superstars!

CHAPTER NINE CHECK-UP

1. As long as you trust your bookkeeper and accountant, it's okay to turn the financial management of the company over to them.

☐ True ☐ False

2. Don't hire an accountant who already works for other remodelers because they may share your information with your competitor.

☐ True ☐ False

3. Name two of the three levels of accounting services.

4. You should take simple precautions to prevent embezzlement—even if you trust your bookkeeper completely.

☐ True ☐ False

5. Always have bank statements sent to your home so that you can review the checks for any discrepancies.

☐ True ☐ False

CHECK YOUR ANSWERS ON THE NEXT PAGE ➜ ➜ ➜

ANSWERS

1. False. You are the financial manager of your company.

2. False. You want to hire an accountant who works for other remodelers because they will already know alot about the industry. They will keep your information completely confidential.

3. The three levels of accounting services are audits, reviews and compilations.

4. True. Even if you trust your bookkeeper completely, take simple precautions against embezzlement.

5. True. Do have bank statements sent to your home and do review them to check for discrepancies.

Chapter 10

Managing by Your Numbers

*"A billion here, a billion there—pretty soon it
adds up to real money."*
Senator Everett Dirksen (1896-1969)

W e've been reviewing the financial reports you need to manage your company for profitability. Perhaps you are discouraged because you are so far away from where you need to be, or because you don't feel you have the money to spend to get these reports. All I can say is you must have them. In purchasing this book, you have made a commitment to getting and managing by your numbers. Professional (profitable) remodeling requires that you have them. So sit down and figure how you will do it and how you'll pay for it. Nothing less will do.

With your monthly Profit & Loss statement, monthly Balance Sheet with ratios, timely job costs, annual budget that creates a roadmap, and accurate reporting from your bookkeeper and accountant, you are ready to mine these gold mines of information for the critical nuggets that will help you shape and guide your company. Let's get going!

What You Want to Know and How to Find Out

Your questions as company owner are really quite simple and logical. All the reports, estimates, ratios and costs we've been discussing are there to answer just such straightforward questions as the following:

1. **IS MY COMPANY MAKING MONEY?**
   Assuming you are using the percentage of completion method of producing your Profit and Loss report, watch your P & L net profit. Also check retained earnings on your balance sheet to be sure that is positive and that you are building earnings over time.

2. **AM I HITTING MY BUDGET GOALS?**
   If not where should we direct our attention to correction?

   Pull out your budget and compare it to where you are on your P & L. Compare these specific categories first—income, job costs, overhead, net profit. Are you on target, behind or ahead? Your budget helps you to zero in on any specific areas that need correction. Have a problem? By revising your budget, you prove—on paper—that you can solve it.

3. **ARE FINANCES IN MY COMPANY GETTING BETTER (OR WORSE)?**
   Here's where having historical data is a real help. Compare the last three years and watch trends. Your P & L's show the company's profitability or lack thereof. Your Balance Sheets will show how your equity is growing or shrinking. Or perhaps you just want to compare the last six months from your P & Ls. You now have the information with which to do it.

4. **WILL I HAVE ENOUGH CASH FLOW OVER THE NEXT MONTH?**

Use your Cash Flow Projector to check how the next month's cash will ebb and flow. By projecting cash income and expense on a spreadsheet or just manually on a legal pad and by including current cash, payables and receivables, you should be able to get a pretty good idea of where you are and where you will be over this relatively short period of time.

5. **AM I PERSONALLY GETTING A GOOD RETURN ON THE MONEY I HAVE INVESTED IN MY COMPANY?**

Here's where your ratios come in handy. Grab your Balance Sheet and check the Return on Equity ratio (net income before taxes divided by net worth/owner's equity) to see if you like the return you are getting compared to what you could achieve by investing elsewhere.

6. **DO I MARK UP MY JOBS ENOUGH?**

Use your annual budget to set the markup percentage for the year. Double check your assumptions with your monthly P & L's. If you're getting an overabundance of leads and potential jobs, raise your markup 5% a month at least, to take advantage of this temporary upswing in the market.

7. **HOW ARE MY JOB COSTS RUNNING COMPARED TO ESTIMATES?**

Now, the value of clear estimates and precise actual job costs becomes important. Check each job individually or, if you want to scan how all your current jobs are doing as a whole, check the job cost summary sheet and the percentage of job costs in your P & L to be sure it matches your targeted percentage on individual jobs.

8. **WHAT KIND OF JOBS SHOULD I BE FOCUSING ON?**

Do some crews produce more profitable jobs than others?

Does any one salesperson have more slippage of gross profit than the others?

Lots of questions—including these—are answered by sorting and resorting information you can gather on your job cost summary sheet.

Author and builder David Gerstel says in *The Builder's Guide to Running a Successful Construction Company*, "The truest foundations, tightest miter joints and closest attention to integrity in human relationships will not save a construction company from poor business management." And a mainstay of that business management is the ability to manage your company based on the numbers you want and the numbers you are getting.

I have a prediction. Once you see how financial information will help you manage your company for profitability, there will be no stopping you. You'll become an information addict—always asking for more and more and more. And that information will help you become more and more profitable and successful.

CHAPTER TEN CHECK-UP

1. What reports would you analyze to find out if a job was coming in on budget?

2. It's July 15, what report(s) would tell you whether you had made a profit in the first six months of the year?

3. Your cash flow projector report will tell you what?

4. How can I check whether the markup I intend to use will actually pay all my bills and leave a net profit?

5. I have left $50,000 in my company, how do I know what return I am getting on it?

CHECK YOUR ANSWERS ON THE NEXT PAGE → → →

ANSWERS

1. You'd analyze how the job cost report compared to the job estimate to find out if a job was coming in on budget.

2. You'd check the Profit and Loss statement for the first six months of the year and look at the net profit line.

3. Your cash flow projector report will tell you whether you will have enough money to pay expected bills and to generate a profit during the time the report covers.

4. First convert your markup to gross profit percentage. Then multiply your expected volume by that percentage to see if the resulting dollar amount will pay for your overhead and your net profit.

5. Use your Balance Sheet to check the Return on Equity that you are getting. Take the net profit from your P & L and divide it by the owner's equity (net worth) to see your return.

Chapter 11

Best of the Best:
Benchmarks of Successful Remodelers

"Money is good for bribing yourself through the inconveniences of life."
Gottfried Reinhardt

What you want to achieve financially in your company is quite clear. **Your company should be consistently solvent and earning net profit to fund future growth while giving you a good return for your risk and effort.** Thus there is little argument about the benchmark, or desired result by which we measure your business financial success. But getting to that "simple" result takes tremendous effort. Let's see how we would measure whether you achieved your goal (measurements) and what key bits of information would be good indicators that you are on the right path. The following measurements come from analyzing financially successful remodelers —that rare breed that comprises less than 5% of remodelers in the country.

We"ll review benchmarks and measurements for:

- owner comfort, and

- financial management

BENCHMARK—THE DESIRED RESULT, THE GOAL, THE KEY ISSUE

Measurements—how a successful remodeler would measure their attainment of that goal.

I **OWNER COMFORT: Owner is happy and comfortable running his/her company over the long term.**

Measurements:

- Pay (in expenses): 10% of volume to $100,000 then add profit sharing, or a minimum of lead carpenter pay plus $5000 — whichever is higher.

- Investment Return: Owner gets a return as an investor in the company which is better than that offered by the investment market and which is commensurate with his/her risk.

- Benefits: health insurance, vehicle, retirement program

- Hours: no more than 55 a week on average

- Leisure: 2-4 weeks vacation

- Role: Owner spends at least 50% of their working time in the role they enjoy most.

■ Owner has high satisfaction level (at least 8 on scale of 10)

■ Owner spends at least 10% of time working **on** company at $250,000

■ Owner spends at least 25% of time working **on** company at $500,000

■ Owner spends at least 90% of time working **on** company at $1.5 million +

II **FINANCIAL MANAGEMENT: Company is consistently solvent and earning a healthy net profit to fund future growth while giving the owner a good return for his/her risk and effort.**

Measurements:

■ The company produces and follows an Annual Budget.

■ The company achieves a net profit of 8% to 10% consistently. The owner's salary is included in either job costs or operating costs.

■ P & L's are generated monthly and are based on accrual method (% of completion).

■ Job costs are targeted to run somewhere in the 60-70% range (64-68% appears prime).**

■ Job cost reports are produced on a timely basis.

■ Job costs are accurate to within 2% of estimate.

■ Overhead runs in the 20-35% range (mid-range is best).**

- Current Ratio (current assets divided by current liabilities) is 1.3:1 or better.

- Quick Ratio (cash + receivables divided by current liabilities) is 1.2:1 or better.

- Debt to Equity Ratio (total assets over total liabilities) is .9:1 or better.

- Return on Equity (net profit before taxes divided by net worth/owner's equity) gives the owner a return as good or better than they could get on their money elsewhere.

** Note: *Companies which specialize in jobs that average $90,000 or more in size, can have higher job costs (near 80%) and a lower overhead (nearer 15%) and still be healthy and profitable. That is because fewer people can produce a greater volume. Thus each dollar of volume carries less overhead.*

This checklist gives you standards to which to aspire. Don't worry if you are only beginning your journey. No remodeler started on top. They've all had to learn at the school of hard knocks. The bad news is that the tuition is very high. The good news is that you'll never forget the lessons you have learned!

Chapter 12

Financial Terms*

Accounts payable: Amount owed to creditors for products and services on an open account.

Accounts receivable: Amount due from customers for products or services purchased on an open account.

Accrual accounting: An accounting method in which revenue is recorded when earned and costs and balance sheet items are recorded when commitments are made.

Asset: Anything owned by a business or individual that has commercial or exchange value.

* This glossary has been adapted from *The Credit Process: A Guide for Small Business Owners* by Tracy L. Penwell, published by The Federal Reserve Bank of New York.

Balance sheet: Financial statement that presents a "snapshot" of what the business owns, what it owes, and what equity it has on a given date.

Capital: Investment in a business.

Capital expenditures: Purchases of long-term assets, such as equipment, that will be accounted for as fixed assets.

Cash accounting: An accounting method in which revenue, costs and balance sheet items are recorded when cash is paid or received.

Cash flow: Incoming cash to the business less the outgoing cash during a given period.

Collateral: Assets pledged to secure a loan.

Collection period ratio: Indicates how quickly your customers pay you. Average accounts receivable divided by net sales, multiplied by 365.

Compensating balance: Money a bank requires a company to leave in a deposit account as part of a loan agreement.

Corporation: Form of business ownership that is a legal entity on its own and puts stockholders and the board of directors in control. Owners have limited liability for the corporation's actions. A corporation has unlimited life and in most cases is taxed as an entity on its own.

Cost of goods sold: Figure representing the cost of buying raw materials and producing finished goods. In most remodelers' P & L's this would be job costs.

Current assets: Cash or other assets you expect to use in the operation of the firm within one year.

Current liabilities: Debts you expect to pay within one year.

Current ratio: Shows the firm's ability to pay its current obligations from current assets. Current assets divided by current liabilities.

Debt: Any liability.

Debt ratio: Indicates the firm's debt level, or leverage. Total liabilities divided by total liabilities plus capital.

Depreciation: Amortization of the cost of a fixed asset, such as plant and equipment, over several years, or the "depreciable life."

Dividend: Distribution of earnings to shareholders.

Equity:	The ownership interest in a business remaining after its liabilities are deducted. Also known as common stock plus retained earnings, or capital.
Extraordinary items:	Unusual or nonrecurring event that must be explained to shareholders or investors, such as a manufacturer's sale of a building.
Financial projections:	Estimates of the future financial performance of a firm.
Financial statements:	Written record of the financial status of an individual or organization. Commonly include profit and loss, or income statement; the balance sheet, which includes a statement of the company's retained earnings; and the cash flow statement.
Fiscal year:	A 12 month period for which financial results are prepared and reported.
Fixed assets:	Long-term assets such as buildings, equipment, or property that are not expected to be converted to cash in the near term.
Generally Accepted Accounting Principles (GAAP):	A set of accounting rules that governs accounting practice.

Gross profit: Indicates the revenues of the firm before consideration of its operating expenses. Net sales less job costs.

Gross profit margin: Measures a firm's profitability. Gross profits divided by net sales.

Inventory: Value of a firm's raw materials, work in process, supplies used in operations, and finished goods.

Investor: An individual who takes an ownership position in a company, thus assuming risk of loss in exchange for anticipated returns.

Leverage: Measures the firm's use of borrowed funds versus those funds provided by the shareholders or owners (equity).

Liability: Something of value owned by a business.

Line of credit: Although not a contract, a bank's promise to lend to a specific borrower up to a pre-agreed amount during a specific time frame. Usually reviewed annually and subject to cancellation without notice.

Liquid assets: Those assets that can be readily turned into cash.

Liquidity: Gauges firm's ability to quickly turn assets into cash.

Margin:	Gross margin is gross profit expressed as a percentage.
Marketable securities:	Securities that are easily sold.
Markup:	The percentage by which job costs are multiplied to obtain selling price.
Net income:	The sum remaining after all expenses have been met or deducted. Also called net profit.
Net worth:	Excess of assets over debt.
Operating expenses:	Those costs associated with the day-to-day activities of the business.
Operating profit (loss):	Income or loss before taxes and extraordinary items resulting from transactions other than those in the normal course of business.
Operating profit margin:	Measures a firm's profitability by examining the pre-tax profit generated from primary operations (versus extraordinary items) in relation to net sales. Operating profit divided by net sales.
Overhead:	Costs associated with production of revenue but not assignable to producing remodeling jobs.
Partnership:	Can be general or limited, but in either case the general partners are in control. The tax burden is shared by

all the partners at their personal rate, and the general partners have unlimited liability. Limited partners have limited liability.

Percentage of completion: Method of accounting that recognizes partial revenue during the length of the contract in the proportion that has been completed.

Principal: The currently unpaid balance of a loan, not including interest owed. Also can refer to a primary owner or investor.

Profit: Compensation an entrepreneur receives for the assumption of risk in a business venture. Also called net income.

Profit and loss statement: Summary of the revenues, costs, and expenses for a business over a period of time. Also called the income statement.

Quick ratio: Liquidity ratio that focuses on the firm's most liquid assets by excluding inventory. Also known as the acid test ratio. Cash, marketable securities, and accounts receivable divided by current liabilities.

Retained earnings: Net profits left to accumulate in a business after dividends are paid.

Shareholders equity: The equity of a corporation.

Sole proprietorship: A type of business where the owner has full control and unlimited liability. A sole proprietorship is taxed at the personal income tax rate.

Variance: The amount by which a cost differs from its budgeted or standard value.

Working capital: Current assets minus current liabilities.

Chapter 13

Keep on Reading!

Bangs, David, **FINANCIAL TROUBLESHOOTING,**
Upstart Publishing, Dover, NH, 1992.
This book covers the financial basics for small businesses
but from the angle of problem solving. It lists the red flags
that should alert the business owner to oncoming difficulty and some practical tips on how to escape financial
hot water.

Case, Linda, **REMODELERS BUSINESS BASICS,** Home
Builder Press, Washington, D.C., 1989.*
A practical, hands-on book on running a successful
remodeling business from A to Z. It includes a substantial 6 chapter section on Company Finances including
cash flow, markup, budgeting, financial reports and
much more.

* Available from *Remodeling Consulting Services, Inc.*, (301-588-8172)

Dickey, Terry, **BUDGETING FOR A SMALL BUSINESS,** The Crisp Small Business and Entrepreneurship Series, Menlo Park, CA, 1994.

A comprehensive guide to planning and budgeting. Dickey covers personal plans, strategic plans, annual budgets, income statement and balance sheet plans.

Finney, Robert G., **EVERY MANAGER'S GUIDE TO BUSINESS FINANCE,** American Management Association, New York, NY, 1994.

A comprehensive rundown on all the ways money flows through a company. It's sophisticated in its tone and focuses on large companies. However, it is an excellent reference book.

Gill, James O., **FINANCIAL BASICS OF SMALL BUSINESS SUCCESS,** The Crisp Small Business and Entrepreneurship Series, Menlo Park, CA, 1994.

An excellent, in depth, graphically clear book on financial reports. Lots of exercises on which to try your own hand.

Halloran, James W., **WHY ENTREPRENEURS FAIL,** Liberty Hall Press, 1991.

Veteran small business advisor covers 20 of the most common traps that await entrepreneurs including: Living off cash flow, not profits; Letting your accountant run the business and Expanding for the wrong reasons.

Lyon, Douglass C., **THE FINANCIAL STATEMENT WORKBOOK,**
Lyco Enterprises, Rochester, NY, 1993.
As advertised, this is a basic tutorial (you work the exercises as you go) on the Balance Sheet, Income Statement and Break-even Analysis.

Penwell, Tracy L., **THE CREDIT PROCESS: A GUIDE FOR SMALL BUSINESS OWNERS,** published by the Federal Reserve Bank of New York, 1994. Available free from the Federal Reserve Bank of Richmond (804-697-8000).
A simply written booklet about the credit process to assist entrepreneurs who are seeking outside financing for the first time—and it's free!

Shinn, Emma, CPA, **ACCOUNTING AND FINANCIAL MANAGEMENT FOR BUILDERS, REMODELERS, AND DEVELOPERS,** Home Builder Press, Washington, D.C, 1993.
The third edition of this book which focuses particularly on builder needs. Shinn does an excellent job of getting from the financial report to the data gathering that leads to accurate reporting.

Stack, Jack, **THE GREAT GAME OF BUSINESS,**
Currency-Doubleday, New York, 1994.
Already the classic on open-book management, Stack covers what happens to a company when all employees —yes, all employees, participate in financial planning and management.